Anonymous

Pearls for Prayer Meetings

and for protracted and revival meetings, and also adapted for family and public worship

Anonymous

Pearls for Prayer Meetings
and for protracted and revival meetings, and also adapted for family and public worship

ISBN/EAN: 9783337286613

Printed in Europe, USA, Canada, Australia, Japan

Cover: Foto ©Lupo / pixelio.de

More available books at **www.hansebooks.com**

Pearls for Prayer Meetings:

PROTRACTED AND REVIVAL MEETINGS,
AND ALSO ADAPTED FOR FAMILY
AND PUBLIC WORSHIP.

BEING A SELECTION OF THE
BEST AND MOST POPULAR HYMNS NOW IN USE.

BY A PASTOR.

NEW YORK:
ANSON D. F. RANDOLPH & CO.,
No. 770 BROADWAY.
Corner of 9th Street.
1869.

PREFACE.

The first edition of this little book was quickly exhausted. and a second is called for. The Press has spoken favorably of it, and many letters have been received from Pastors who have carefully examined it, speaking of it in terms of unqualified approbation, as meeting a great want in the Church.

In view of the fact also that our approved hymn books are all expensive, many ministers strongly advised that a few additional hymns should be added to this collection, so that the book may be adapted not merely to private and family worship, and to prayer meetings, but also to the public services of the sanctuary on the Lord's day, and may be used exclusively, especially in new and feeble congregations, where the people are unable to supply themselves with larger and more costly books.

Twenty-six additional hymns have. therefore, been added on the following subjects, viz: Morning, Children and Youth. The Sabbath, 'The Church, Public Worship, The Lord's Sup-

PREFACE.

per, The Gospel Ministry, and The Bible, so that now, small as the book is, it contains one or more hymns adapted to almost every subject.

Those who use the book will find it a great advantage to have the hymns always sung to the same tunes; when this is done it is found by experience, that it tends greatly to promote the general singing of the congregation, and thus to increase the interest of worship.

A few unimportant errors in the first edition have been corrected, and the little volume is now sent forth with the humble hope that it will aid God's people in his worship, and promote the salvation of souls.

Pearls for Prayer Meetings.

CHRIST.

1.   ANTIOCH.   C. M.

Joy to the world the Lord is come,
   Let earth receive her King;
Let every heart prepare Him room,
   And heaven and nature sing.

Joy to the earth, the Saviour reigns;
   Let men their songs employ,
While fields and floods, rocks, hills and plains
   Repeat the sounding joy.

No more let sins and sorrows grow,
   Nor thorns infest the ground;
He comes to make His blessings flow
   Far as the curse is found.

He rules the world with truth and grace,
   And makes the nations prove
The glories of His righteousness,
   And wonders of His love.

2.   CORONATION.   C. M.

All hail the power of Jesus' name!
  Let angels prostrate fall,
Bring forth the royal diadem,
  And crown Him Lord of all.

Ye chosen seed of Israel's race,
  Ye ransomed from the fall,
Hail Him, who saves you by His grace,
  And crown Him Lord of all.

Sinners, whose love can ne'er forget
  The wormwood and the gall,
Go, spread your trophies at His feet,
  And crown Him Lord of all.

Let every kindred, every tribe,
  On this terrestrial ball,
To Him all majesty ascribe,
  And crown Him Lord of all.

Oh that with yonder sacred throng,
  We at His feet may fall;
We'll join the everlasting song,
  And crown Him Lord of all.

3.   MARLOW. C. M.

Oh! for a thousand tongues to sing
  My dear Redeemer's praise;
The glories of my God and King,
  The triumphs of His grace.

My gracious Master, and my God,
  Assist me to proclaim,
To spread through all the earth abroad
  The honors of Thy name.

Jesus, the name that calms our fears,
  That bids our sorrows cease.
'Tis music in the sinner's ears,
  'Tis life, and health, and peace.

He breaks the power of reigning sin,
  He sets the pris'ner free;
His blood can make the foulest clean,
  His blood availed for me.

4. ELIZABETHTOWN, OR ORTONVILLE. C. M.

How sweet the name of Jesus sounds
  In a believer's ear!
It soothes his sorrows, heals his wounds,
  And drives away his fear.

It makes the wounded spirit whole,
   And calms the troubled breast;
'Tis manna to the hungry soul,
   And to the weary rest.

Dear Name the rock on which I build,
   My shield and hiding-place;
My never-failing treas'ry, filled
   With boundless stores of grace.

Weak is the effort of my heart,
   And cold my warmest thought;
But when I see Thee as Thou art,
   I'll praise Thee as I ought.

Till then I would Thy love proclaim
   With every fleeting breath;
And may the music of Thy name
   Refresh my soul in death.

5. THE SWEETEST NAME, OR THE NAME OF JESUS.

There is no name so sweet on earth,
   No name so sweet in heaven,
The name before his wondrous birth
   To Christ the Saviour given.

CHORUS. We love to sing around our King,
            And hail him blessed Jesus;
            For there's no word ear ever heard
               So dear, so sweet, as Jesus.

His human name they did proclaim
    When Abr'am's son they sealed him,
The name that still, by God's good will
    Deliverer revealed him.   CHORUS.

And when he hung upon the tree,
    They wrote this name above him,
That all might see the reason we
    Forevermore must love him.   CHORUS.

So now upon his Father's throne,
    Almighty to release us
From sins and pains, he gladly reigns,
    The Prince and Saviour Jesus.   CHORUS.

To Jesus every knee shall bow
    And every tongue confess him,
And we unite with saints in light,
    Our only Lord to bless him.   CHORUS.

O Jesus, by thy matchless name,
    Thy grace shall fail us never;
To-day as yesterday the same,
    Thou art the same forever.   CHORUS.

6. TOPLADY, OR "ROCK OF AGES." 7's.

Rock of Ages, cleft for me
Let me hide myself in Thee;
Let the water and the blood
From Thy wounded side which flowed,

Be of sin the double cure,—
Cleanse me from its guilt and pow'r.

Not the labor of my hands
Can fulfil the law's demands;
Could my zeal no respite know
Could my tears forever flow,
All for sin could not atone,—
Thou must save, and Thou alone.

Nothing in my hand' I bring;
Simply to Thy cross I cling;
Naked, come to Thee for dress,
Helpless, look to Thee for grace,—
Vile, I to the fountain fly,
Wash me, Saviour, or I die.

While I draw this fleeting breath,
When my heart-strings break in death,
When I soar to worlds unknown,
See Thee on Thy judgment throne,—
Rock of Ages, cleft for me,
Let me hide myself in Thee.

7.   ARIEL.   L. C. M.

OH could I speak the matchless worth,
Oh could I sound the glories forth,
    Which in my Saviour shine;
I'd soar and touch the heavenly strings,
And vie with Gabriel, while he sings,
    In notes almost divine.

I'd sing the precious blood He spilt,
My ransom from the dreadful guilt
  Of sin and wrath divine;
I'd sing his glorious righteousness,
In which all-perfect, heavenly dress
  My soul shall ever shine.

I'd sing the characters He bears,
And all the forms of love He wears,
  Exalted on His throne;
In loftiest songs of sweetest praise,
I would to everlasting days
  Make all His glories known.

Soon the delightful day will come,
When my dear Lord will call me home,
  And I shall see His face:
Then with my Saviour, Brother, Friend,
A blest eternity I'll spend,
  Triumphant in His grace.

8.   AZMON, OR EVAN. C. M.

The Saviour! oh what endless charms
  Dwell in the blissful sound;
Its influence every fear disarms,
  And spreads sweet comfort round.

Th' Almighty Former of the skies
  Stooped to our vile abode;
While angels viewed with wondering eyes,
  And hailed th' incarnate God.

Oh the rich depth of love divine!
  Of bliss a boundless store!
Dear Saviour let me call Thee mine,
  I cannot wish for more.

On Thee alone my hope relies,
  Beneath Thy cross I fall;
My Lord, my Life, my Sacrifice,
  My Saviour, and my all.

9. NAOMI, OR WOODLAND. C. M.

Dearest of all the names above,
  My Jesus, and my God,
Who can resist Thy heav'nly love
  Or trifle with Thy blood?

'Tis by the merits of Thy death
  The Father smiles again;
'Tis by Thine interceding breath
  The Spirit dwells with men.

Till God in human flesh I see,
  My thoughts no comfort find;
The holy, just, and sacred Three
  Are terrors to my mind.

But, if Immanuel's face appear,
  My hope, my joy begins,
His name forbids my slavish fear,
  His grace removes my sins.

While Jews on their own law rely,
  And Greeks of wisdom boast,
I love th' incarnate mystery,
  And there I fix my trust.

10.   DORRANCE.   8, 7.

One there is above all others
  Well deserves the name of Friend;
His is love beyond a brother's,
  Costly, free, and knows no end.

Which of all our friends, to save us,
  Could or would have shed his blood?
But this Saviour died to have us,
  Reconciled in Him to God.

When He lived on earth abased,
  Friend of sinners was His name;
Now, above all glory raised,
  He rejoices in the same.

Oh for grace our hearts to soften,
  Teach us, Lord, at length to love;
We, alas! forget too often
  What a Friend we have above.

11.   EVAN, OR BROWN.   C. M.

Didst Thou, dear Jesus, suffer shame,
  And bear the cross for me?
And shall I fear to own Thy name,
  Or Thy disciple be?

Forbid it, Lord, that I should dread
  To suffer shame or loss;
Oh let me in Thy footsteps tread,
  And glory in Thy cross.

Say to my soul, "Why dost thou fear
  The face of feeble clay?
Behold thy Saviour ever near
  Will guard thee in the way."

Oh how my soul would rise and run
  At this reviving word,
Nor any painful suff'rings shun,
  To follow Thee, my Lord.

Let sinful men reproach, defame,
  And call me what they will,—
If I may glorify Thy name,
  And be Thy servant still.

12. ELIZABETHTOWN, OR WOODLAND. C. M.

JESUS, I love Thy charming name,
  'Tis music to mine ear;
Fain would I sound it out so loud
  That earth and heaven should hear.

Yes, Thou art precious to my soul,
  My joy, my hope, my trust;
Jewels to Thee, are gaudy toys,
  And gold is sordid dust.

All my capacious powers can wish
   In Thee most richly meet;
Nor to mine eyes is light so dear,
   Nor friendship half so sweet.

Thy grace still dwells upon my heart,
   And sheds its fragrance there,
The noblest balm of all its wounds,
   The cordial of its care.

I'll speak the honors of Thy name
   With my last lab'ring breath;
Then speechless clasp Thee in mine arms,
   The antidote of death.

13. NOTTING HILL, OR RIDGWOOD. C. M.

   I saw one hanging on a tree,
      In agonies and blood,
   Who fixed His languid eyes on me,
      As near His cross I stood.

   Sure, never to my latest breath
      Can I forget that look;
   It seemed to charge me with His death,
      Though not a word He spoke.

   A second look He gave, which said
      "I freely all forgive;
   This blood is for thy ransom paid,
      I die, that Thou may'st live."

Thus, while His death my sin displays
  In all its blackest hue;
Such is the myst'ry of grace,
  It seals my pardon too.

With pleasing grief and mournful joy
  My spirit now is filled;
That I should such a life destroy,
  Yet live by Him I killed.

14. NEANDER, OR KENTUCKY. S. M.

Not all the blood of beasts,
  On Jewish altars slain,
Could give the guilty conscience peace,
Or wash away the stain.

But Christ, the heav'nly Lamb,
  Takes all our sins away,—
A sacrifice of nobler name,
  And richer blood than they.

My faith would lay her hand
  On that dear head of Thine,
While like a penitent I stand,
  And there confess my sin.

My soul looks back to see
  The burdens Thou didst bear,
When hanging on the cursed tree,
  And hopes her guilt was there.

15.   LIBERTY HALL.   C. M.

Dark was the night, and cold the ground,
  On which the Lord was laid;
His sweat as drops of blood ran down,
  In agony he prayed.

"Father, remove this bitter cup,
  If such thy sacred will;
If not, content to drink it up,
  Thy pleasure I fulfil."

Go to the garden, sinner, see
  Those precious drops that flow:
The heavy load he bore for thee—
  For thee he lies so low.

Then learn of him the cross to bear,
  Thy Father's will obey;
And when temptations press thee near,
  Awake to watch and pray.

16.   MARTYN, 7's, DOUBLE.

Jesus, lover of my soul,
  Let me to Thy bosom fly,
While the billows near me roll,
  While the tempest still is high:
Hide me, O my Saviour, hide,
  Till the storm of life is past,
Safe into the haven guide;
  O receive my soul at last.

Other refuge have I none,
    Hangs my helpless soul on Thee;
Leave, ah! leave me not alone,
    Still support and comfort me;
All my trust on Thee is stayed,
    All my help from Thee I bring;
Cover my defenceless head
    With the shadow of Thy wing.

Thou, O Christ, art all I want,
    All in all in Thee I find;
Raise the fallen, cheer the faint,
    Heal the sick, and lead the blind:
Just and holy is Thy name,
    I am all unrighteousness;
Vile and full of sin I am,
    Thou art full of truth and grace.

Plenteous grace with Thee is found,
    Grace to pardon all my sin;
Let the healing streams abound,
    Make and keep me pure within:
Thou of life the fountain art,
    Freely let me take of Thee;
Spring thou up within my heart,—
    Rise to all eternity.

17. AYLESBURY, OR GOLDEN HILL. S. M.

Did Christ o'er sinners weep?
And shall our cheeks be dry?

Let floods of penitential grief
 Burst forth from every eye.

The Son of God in tears
 Angels with wonder see;
Be thou astonished, O my soul,
 He shed those tears for thee.

He wept that we might weep;
 Each sin demands a tear:
In heaven alone no sin is found,
 And there's no weeping there.

18. OLD HUNDRED. L. M.

Nature with open volume stands
 To spread her Maker's praise abroad,
And every labor of His hands
 Shows something worthy of a God.

But in the grace that rescued man
 His brightest form of glory shines;
Here, on the cross, 'tis fairest drawn,
 In precious blood and crimson lines.

Oh the sweet wonders of that cross,
 Where God the Saviour loved and died;
Her noblest life my spirit draws
 From His dear wounds and bleeding side.

I would for ever speak His name
  In sounds to mortal ears unknown;
With angels join to praise the Lamb,
  And worship at His Father's throne.

19. DUNLAP'S CREEK OR MARLOW. C. M.

PLUNGED in a gulf of dark despair,
  We wretched sinners lay,
Without one cheerful beam of hope,
  Or spark of glimm'ring day.

With pitying eyes the Prince of grace
  Beheld our helpless grief;
He saw, and, oh amazing love
  He ran to our relief.

Down from the shining seats above
  With joyful haste He fled,
Entered the grave in mortal flesh,
  And dwelt among the dead.

He spoiled the powers of darkness thus
  And brake our iron chains;
Jesus has freed our captive souls
  From everlasting pains.

Oh! for this love let rocks and hills
  Their lasting silence break;
And all harmonious human tongues
  The Saviour's praises speak.

CHRIST.

20. TOPLADY, OR "ROCK OF AGES." 7's.

From the cross uplifted high,
Where the Saviour deigns to die,
What melodious sounds I hear,
Bursting on my ravished ear!
Love's redeeming work is done,
"Come and welcome, sinner, come.

"Sprinkled now with blood the throne,
Why beneath thy burdens groan?
On My pierced body laid,
Justice owns the ransom paid;
Bow the knee and kiss the Son,
Come and welcome, sinner, come.

"Spread for thee the festal board,
See with richest dainties stored;
To thy Father's bosom pressed,
Yet again a child confessed,
Never from His house to roam,
Come and welcome, sinner, come.

"Soon the days of life shall end,
Lo! I come, your Saviour, Friend,
Safe your spirits to convey
To the realms of endless day:
Up to My eternal home.
Come and welcome, sinner, come."

21. FOUNT, OR GOOD SHEPHERD, OR
MIDDLETON. 8, 7.

Jesus, full of all compassion,
　Hear Thy humble suppliant's cry,—
Let me know thy great salvation;
　See, I languish, faint, and die:
Guilty, but with heart relenting,
　Overwhelmed with helpless grief,
Prostrate at Thy feet repenting,
　Send, oh send me quick relief.

Whither should a wretch be flying,
　But to Him who comfort gives?
Whither, from the dread of dying,
　But to Him who ever lives?
While I view Thee, wounded, grieving,
　Breathless on the cursed tree,
Fain, I'd feel my heart believing
　That Thou suffer'dst thus for me.

With Thy righteousness and Spirit
　I am more than angels blessed;
Heir with Thee, all things inherit,
　Peace, and joy, and endless rest:
Saved!—the deed shall spread new glory
　Through the shining realms above;
Angels sing the pleasing story,
　All enraptured with Thy love.

22.   AYLESBURY.   S. M.

Like sheep we went astray,
  And broke the fold of God;
Each wandering in a different way,
  But all the downward road.

How dreadful was the hour,
  When God our wanderings laid,
And did at once his vengeance pour
  Upon the Shepherd's head!

How glorious was the grace
  When Christ sustained the stroke!
His life and blood the Shepherd pays
  A ransom for the flock.

But God shall raise his head
  O'er all the sons of men,
And make him see a numerous seed,
  To recompense his pain.

"I'll give him," saith the Lord,
  "A portion with the strong;
He shall possess a large reward,
  And hold his honors long."

23.   HAMBURG.   L. M.

When I survey the wondrous cross,
  On which the Prince of glory died,

My richest gain I count but loss,
  And pour contempt on all my pride.
Forbid it, Lord, that I should boast,
  Save in the death of Christ, my God;
All the vain things that charm me most,
  I sacrifice them to His blood.

See! from His head, His hands, His feet,
  Sorrow and love flow mingled down;
Did e'er such love and sorrow meet,
  Or thorns compose so rich a crown?

His dying crimson, like a robe,
  Spreads o'er His body on the tree;
Then am I dead to all the globe,
  And all the globe is dead to me.

Were the whole realm of nature mine,
  That were a present far too small;
Love so amazing, so divine,
  Demands my soul, my life, my all.

24. BALERMA, OR SUFFERING SAVIOUR.
C. M. WITH CHORUS.

Alas! and did my Saviour bleed,
  And did my Sov'reign die?
Would He devote that sacred head
  For such a worm as I?

CHORUS.

O the Lamb, the loving Lamb,
  The Lamb on calvary—
The Lamb that was slain, that liveth again
  To intercede for me.

Thy body slain, dear Jesus, Thine,—
  And bathed in its own blood;
While all exposed to wrath divine
  The glorious sufferer stood.

Was it for crimes that I had done,
  He groaned upon the tree?
Amazing pity! grace unknown!
  And love beyond degree!

Well might the sun in darkness hide,
  And shut his glories in,
When God, the mighty Maker, died
  For man, the creature's sin.

Thus might I hide my blushing face,
  While His dear cross appears,
Dissolve my heart in thankfulness,
  And melt my eyes to tears.

But drops of grief can ne'er repay
  The debt of love I owe;
Here, Lord, I give myself away,
  'Tis all that I can do.

25. FOUNTAIN, OR CLEANSING FOUNTAIN. C. M.

There is a fountain filled with blood,
  Drawn from Immanuel's veins,
And sinners plunged beneath that flood
  Lose all their guilty stains.

The dying thief rejoiced to see
  That fountain in his day;
And there may I, though vile as he,
  Wash all my sins away.

Dear dying Lamb, Thy precious blood
  Shall never lose its power,
Till all the ransomed church of God
  Be saved to sin no more.

E'er since by faith, I saw the stream,
  Thy flowing wounds supply,
Redeeming love has been my theme,
  And shall be till I die.

Then, in a nobler, sweeter song,
  I'll sing Thy power to save,
When this poor lisping, stamm'ring tongue
  Lies silent in the grave.

HOLY SPIRIT.

26. HEBER, OR HARMONY GROVE. C. M

Come, Holy Spirit, heavenly Dove,
  With all Thy quick'ning powers,
Kindle a flame of sacred love
  In these cold hearts of ours.

Look how we grovel here below,
　　Fond of these trifling toys;
Our souls can neither fly nor go
　　To reach eternal joys.

In vain we tune our formal songs,
　　In vain we strive to rise;
Hosannas languish on our tongues,
　　And our devotion dies.

Dear Lord and shall we ever live
　　At this poor dying rate,
Our love so faint, so cold to Thee,
　　And Thine to us so great?

Come, Holy Spirit, heavenly Dove,
　　With all Thy quick'ning powers,
Come, shed abroad a Saviour's love
　　And that shall kindle ours.

27.　　　STATE STREET.　S. M.

Come, Holy Spirit, come,
　　Let Thy bright beams arise;
Dispel the darkness from our minds,
　　And open Thou our eyes.

Revive our drooping faith,
　　Our doubts and fears remove,
And kindle in our breasts the flame
　　Of never-dying love.

Convince us of our sin,
  Then lead to Jesus' blood;
And to our wond'ring view reveal
  The gracious love of God.

'Tis Thine to cleanse the heart,
  To sanctify the soul,
To pour fresh life on every part,
  And new create the whole.

Dwell, therefore, in our hearts,
  Our minds from bondage free;
Then shall we know, and praise, and love
  The Father, Son, and Thee.

28.   TELLEMAN. 7'S, OR HORTON.

Holy Ghost, with light divine
Shine upon this heart of mine;
Chase the shades of night away,
Turn my darkness into day.

Holy Ghost, with power divine
Cleanse this guilty heart of mine;
Long hath sin, without control,
Held dominion o'er my soul.

Holy Ghost, with joy divine
Cheer this saddened heart of mine;
Bid my many woes depart,
Heal my wounded, bleeding heart.

Holy Spirit, all divine,
Dwell within this heart of mine,
Cast down every idol throne,
Reign supreme, and reign alone.

29. OBERLIN. L. M.

Come, sacred Spirit, from above,
And fill the coldest heart with love;
Soften to flesh the flinty stone,
And let Thy God-like power be known.

Speak Thou, and from the haughtiest eyes
Shall floods of pious sorrow rise,
While all their glowing souls are borne,
To seek that grace which now they scorn.

O let a holy flock await
Numerous around Thy temple-gate;
Each pressing on with zeal to be
A living sacrifice to Thee.

In answer to our fervent cries,
Give us to see Thy church arise;
Or, if that blessing seem too great,
Give us to mourn its low estate.

30. GREENVILLE 8, 7, 4, OR FOUNT.

Saviour, visit Thy plantation,
  Grant us, Lord, a gracious rain;
All will come to desolation,

Unless Thou return again.
   Lord, revive us;
All our help must come from Thee.

Let our mutual love be fervent,
   Make us prevalent in prayers;
Let each one, esteemed Thy servant,
   Shun the world's bewitching snares.
      Lord, revive us;
All our help must come from Thee.

31.   HORTON, OR FULTON, 7's.

Lord, behold us few and weak,
   Humbly at Thy feet we fall;
See, we come Thy face to seek,
   Deign, oh deign to hear our call.

When we lay in sin and death,
   Thou didst pass and bid us live,
Thou didst give Thy people faith,
   Thou didst all our sins forgive.

Jesus, Thou didst shed Thy blood,
   On this rock our hope we raise,
Thou hast brought us near to God,
   Thine the work, and Thine the praise

'Tis Thy will that we should be
   Separate from all around,
Let our will with Thine agree,
   Let Thy people thus be found.

Let us bear each other's load,
   Faithful to each other prove,
Till we gain the saints' abode,
   Till we take our place above.

There to see without a cloud,
   There with zeal untired to sing,
Mix with heaven's triumphant crowd,
   And for ever praise our King.

32.   PARAH. S. M.

O Lord! thy work revive
   In Zion's gloomy hour;
And let our dying graces live,
   By thy restoring power.

O let thy chosen few
   Awake to earnest prayer;
Their solemn vows again renew,
   And walk in filial fear.

Thy Spirit then will speak,
   Through lips of humble clay,
Till hearts of adamant shall break,—
   Till rebels shall obey.

Now lend thy gracious ear,
   Now listen to our cry;
O come, and bring salvation near;
   Our souls on thee rely.

SINNERS INVITED AND EXHORTED.

33.   AZMON.   C. M.

The Saviour calls, let every ear
 Attend the heavenly sound;
Ye doubting souls, dismiss your fear,
 Hope smiles reviving round.

For every thirsty, longing heart,
 Here streams of bounty flow;
And life, and health, and bliss impart,
 To banish mortal woe.

Here springs of sacred pleasure rise,
 To ease your every pain;
Immortal fountain! full supplies!
 Nor shall you thirst in vain.

Ye sinners come, 'tis Mercy's voice,
 The gracious call obey:
Mercy invites to heavenly joys,
 And can you yet delay?

Dear Saviour, draw reluctant hearts;
 To thee let sinners fly,
And take the bliss thy love imparts,
 And drink and never die.

34. HARMONY GROVE. C. M.

Ye wretched, hungry, starving poor,
    Behold a royal feast:
Where mercy spreads her bounteous store,
    For every humble guest.

See, Jesus stands with open arms,
    He calls, he bids you come;
Guilt holds you back, and fear alarms;
    But see, there yet is room.

Room in the Saviour's bleeding heart,
    There love and pity meet;
Nor will he bid the soul depart,
    That trembles at his feet.

O! come, and with his children taste
    The blessings of his love:
While hope attends the sweet repast
    Of nobler joys above.

35. WOODSTOCK. C. M.

Let every mortal ear attend,
    And every heart rejoice;
The trumpet of the gospel sounds,
    With an inviting voice.

Ho! all ye hungry, starving souls,
    That feed upon the wind,

And vainly strive with earthly toys
  To fill an empty mind:

Eternal wisdom has prepared
  A soul reviving feast,
And bids your longing appetites,
  The rich provision taste.

Ho! ye that pant for living streams,
  And pine away and die,
Here you may quench your raging thirst,
  With springs that never dry.

Rivers of love and mercy here
  In a rich ocean join;
Salvation in abundance flows,
  Like floods of milk and wine.

36. ALETTA, 7, 6, OR ROCK OF AGES.

Ye who in His courts are found,
Listening to the joyful sound,
Lost and helpless as ye are,
Full of sorrow, sin, and care,
Glorify the King of kings;
Take the peace the gospel brings.

Turn to Christ your longing eyes,
View His bleeding sacrifice;

See in Him your sins forgiven,
Pardon, holiness, and heaven;
Glorify the King of kings,
Take the peace the gospel brings.

37.   HARMONY GROVE.   C. M.

Oh! what amazing words of grace
  Are in the gospel found,
Suited to every sinner's case
  Who hears the joyful sound!

Come, then, with all your wants and wounds,
  Your every burden bring;
Here love, unchanging love abounds,
  A deep celestial spring.

This spring with living waters flows,
  And heavenly joys imparts;
Come, thirsty souls! your wants disclose,
  And drink with thankful hearts.

Millions of sinners, vile as you,
  Have here found life and peace;
Come, then, and prove its virtues too,
  And drink, adore, and bless.

38.   AMOY.   P. M.

To-day the Saviour calls:
Ye wanderers, come!

O ye benighted souls,
Why longer roam?

To-day the Saviour calls:
O listen now!
Within these sacred walls,
To Jesus bow.

To-day the Saviour calls;
For refuge fly:
The storm of justice falls,
And death is nigh.

The Spirit calls to-day:
Yield to his power;
O grieve him not away!
'Tis mercy's hour.

39. WELTON. L. M.

Behold a stranger at the door!
He gently knocks, has knocked before;
Has waited long—is waiting still;
You treat no other friend so ill.

O lovely attitude, he stands
With melting heart and bleeding hands.
O matchless kindness, and he shows
This matchless kindness to his foes!

But will he prove a Friend indeed!
He will—the very Friend you need;

The friend of sinners—yes, 'tis He,
With garments dyed on Calvary.

Rise, touched with gratitude divine;
Turn out his enemy and thine,
That soul-destroying monster sin,
And let the heavenly stranger in.

Admit him, ere his anger burn;
His feet departed ne'er return;
Admit him, or the hour's at hand,
You'll at his door rejected stand.

40.   AVA, OR TO-DAY.   P. M.

Child of sin and sorrow,
Filled with dismay,
Wait not for to-morrow,
Yield thee to-day:
Heaven bids thee come,
While yet there's room;
Child of sin and sorrow,
Hear and obey.

Child of sin and sorrow,
Why wilt thou die!
Come while thou canst borrow
Help from on high:
Grieve not that love,
Which from above,
Child of sin and sorrow,
Would bring thee nigh.

41.   HORTON, 7's.

Come! said Jesus' sacred voice,
Come, and make my paths your choice:
I will guide you to your home:
Weary wanderer, hither come.

Thou who homeless and forlorn,
Long hast borne the proud world's scorn,
Long hast roamed the barren waste,
Weary wanderer, hither haste.

Ye who tossed on beds of pain
Seek for ease, but seek in vain;
Ye, by fiercer anguish torn,
In remorse for guilt who mourn:

Hither come, for here is found
Balm that flows for every wound!
Peace that ever shall endure,
Rest eternal, sacred, sure.

42.   FREDERICK, 11's.

Delay not, delay not; O sinner, draw near,
  The waters of life are now flowing for thee;
No price is demanded, the Saviour is here,
  Redemption is purchased, salvation is free.

SINNERS INVITED AND EXHORTED. 37

Delay not, delay not; why longer abuse
  The love and compassion of Jesus, thy
    God?
A fountain is opened—how canst thou re-
    fuse
  To wash and be cleansed in his pardon-
    ing blood?

Delay not, delay not, O sinner to come,
  For mercy still lingers and calls thee to-
    day;
Her voice is not heard in the vale of the
    tomb,—
  Her message, unheeded, will soon pass
    away.

Delay not, delay not; the Spirit of grace,
  Long grieved and resisted, may take its
    sad flight;
And leave thee in darkness to finish thy
    race,—
  To sink in the gloom of eternity's night.

43. GREENVILLE, 8, 7, 4, OR FOUNT.

Come, ye sinners, poor and wretched,
  Weak and wounded, sick and sore,
Jesus ready stands to save you,
  Full of pity, love and power:
    He is able,
  He is willing; doubt no more.

Ho! ye needy, come and welcome,
   God's free bounty glorify;
True belief and true repentance,
   Every grace that brings us nigh,
     Without money,
Come to Jesus Christ and buy.

Let not conscience make you linger,
   Nor of fitness fondly dream;
All the fitness he requireth,
   Is to feel your need of him;
     This he gives you;
'Tis the Spirit's rising beam.

Come, ye weary, heavy laden,
   Lost and ruined by the fall;
If you tarry till you're better,
   You will never come at all.
     Not the righteous,
Sinners Jesus came to call.

Agonizing in the garden,
   Lo! your Maker prostrate lies;
On the bloody tree behold him;
   Hear him cry, before he dies:
     "It is finished!"
Sinner, will not this suffice?

Lo! the incarnate God ascended,
   Pleads the merits of his blood;
Venture to him, venture wholly,

SINNERS INVITED AND EXHORTED. 39

 Let no other trust intrude;
  None but Jesus
 Can do helpless sinners good.

44. PLEADING SAVIOUR, 8, 7.

Now the Saviour standeth pleading
 At the sinner's bolted heart;
Now in heav'n he's interceding,
 Taking there the sinner's part:

Sinner! can you hate this Saviour?
 Will you thrust him from your arms?
Once he died through your behavior,
 Now he calls you by his charms.

Sinner! hear your God and Saviour,
 Hear his gracious voice to-day,
Turn from all your vain behavior,
 Oh! repent, return, and pray!

Now he's waiting to be gracious,
 Now he stands and looks on thee:
See what kindness, love, and pity,
 Shine around on you and me.

45. WARD. L. M.

Say, sinner, hath a voice within,
Oft whispered to thy secret soul:
Urged thee to leave the ways of sin,
And yield thy heart to God's control.?

Hath something met thee in the path
Of worldliness and vanity,
And pointed to the coming wrath,
And warned thee from that wrath to flee?

Sinner, it was a heavenly voice,
It was the Spirit's gracious call;
It bade thee make the better choice,
And hast to seek in Christ thine all.

Spurn not the call to life and light;
Regard in time the warning kind;
That call thou mayst not always slight,
And yet the gate of mercy find.

God's Spirit will not always strive
With hardened, self-destroying man;
Ye who persist his love to grieve,
May never hear his voice again.

Sinner, perhaps this very day,
Thy last accepted time may be;
O shouldst thou grieve him now away,
Then hope may never beam on thee.

46.   WELTON.   L. M.

Return, O wanderer, return,
And seek an injured Father's face;
Those warm desires that in thee burn,
Were kindled by reclaiming grace.

SINNERS INVITED AND EXHORTED.

Return, O wanderer, return,
And seek a Father's melting heart;
His pitying eyes thy grief discern,
His hand shall heal thine inward smart.

Return, O wanderer, return,
Thy Saviour bids thy spirit live;
Go to his bleeding feet and learn
How freely Jesus can forgive.

Return, O wanderer, return,
And wipe away the falling tear;
'Tis God who says, "No longer mourn."
'Tis mercy's voice invites thee near.

47.   AZMON. C. M.

Return, O wanderer, to thy home,
  Thy Father calls for thee;
No longer now an exile roam
  In guilt and misery.

Return, O wanderer, to thy home,
  'Tis Jesus calls for thee.
The Spirit and the bride say, Come!
  Oh now for refuge flee.

Return, O wanderer, to thy home,
  'Tis madness to delay:

There are no pardons in the tomb,
  And brief is mercy's day.

48. IOWA, OR KENTUCKY. S. M.

Now is th' accepted time,
  Now is the day of grace;
O sinners! come, without delay,
  And seek the Saviour's face.

Now is th' accepted time,
  The Saviour calls to-day;
To-morrow it may be too late;
  Then why should you delay.

Now is th' accepted time,
  The Gospel bids you come;
And every promise in his word,
  Declares there yet is room.

Lord! draw reluctant souls,
  And melt them by thy love;
Then will the angels speed their way,
  To bear the news above.

49. BALERMA. C. M.

Come, humble sinner, in whose breast,
  A thousand thoughts revolve;

Come, with your guilt and fear oppressed,
   And make this last resolve:

"I'll go to Jesus, though my sin
   High as a mountain rose;
I know his courts, I'll enter in,
   Whatever may oppose.

"Prostrate I'll lie before his throne,
   And there my guilt confess;
I'll tell him I'm a wretch undone
   Without his sovereign grace.

"I'll to the gracious King approach,
   Whose sceptre pardon give;
Perhaps he may command my touch,
   And then the suppliant lives.

"Perhaps he will admit my plea,
   Perhaps will hear my prayer;
But if I perish, I will pray
   And perish only there.

"I can but perish if I go,
   I am resolved to try;
For if I stay away, I know
   I must for ever die."

50.   MARTYN, 7's, DOUBLE.

Sinners, turn, why will ye die?
God your Maker asks you why;

God who did your being give,
Made you with himself to live,
He the fatal cause demands,
Asks the work of his own hands;
Why, ye thankless creatures, why
Will ye cross his love and die?

Sinners, turn, why will ye die?
God your Saviour asks you why;
He who did your souls retrieve,
Died himself that ye might live,
Will ye let him die in vain,
Crucify your Lord again?
Why, ye rebel sinners, why
Will ye slight his grace and die?

Sinners, turn, why will ye die?
God the Spirit asks you why;
Many a time with you he strove,
Wooed you to embrace his love;
Will ye not his grace receive?
Will ye still refuse to live?
Why will ye for ever die,
O ye guilty sinners, why?

51. HORTON, OR FULTON. 7's.

Brother, hast thou wandered far
  From thy Father's happy home,
With thyself and God at war?
  Turn thee, brother; homeward come

Hast thou wasted all the powers
　　God for noble uses gave?
Squandered life's most golden hours?
　　Turn thee, brother; God can save.

He can heal thy bitterest wound,
　　He thy gentlest prayer can hear;
Seek him, for he may be found;
　　Call upon him; he is near.

52.　　　OLNEY.　S. M.

The Spirit in our hearts,
　　Is whisp'ring, Sinner, Come;
The bride, the church of Christ, proclaims,
　　To all his children, Come.

Let him that heareth say
　　To all about him, Come;
Let him that thirsts for righteousness,
　　To Christ, the fountain, come.

Yes, whosoever will,
　　Oh! let him freely come,
And freely drink the stream of life,
　　'Tis Jesus bids him come.

Lo, Jesus, who invites,
　　Declares, I quickly come:
Lord, even so! we wait thy hour;
　　O blest Redeemer, come!

THE SINNER REPENTING.

53. PENITENT, OR WINDHAM. L. M.

O Thou, that hear'st when sinners cry,
Though all my crimes before Thee lie,
Behold them not with angry look,
But blot their mem'ry from Thy book.

Create my nature pure within,
And form my soul averse to sin;
Let Thy good Spirit ne'er depart,
Nor hide Thy presence from my heart.

I cannot live without Thy light,
Cast out and banished from Thy sight;
Thy holy joys, my God, restore,
And guard me that I fall no more.

Though I have grieved Thy Spirit, Lord,
Thy help and comfort still afford,
And let a wretch come near Thy throne,
To plead the merits of Thy Son.

54. PENITENT. L. M.

Stay, Thou insulted Spirit, stay;
　Though I have done Thee such despite,
Cast not the sinner quite away,
　Nor take Thine everlasting flight.

Though I have most unfaithful been
  Of all, who e'er Thy grace received,
Ten thousand times Thy goodness seen,
  Ten thousand times Thy goodness grieved:

Yet oh, the chief of sinners spare,
  In honor of my great High Priest;
Nor in Thy righteous anger swear,
  I shall not see Thy people's rest.

If yet Thou canst my sins forgive,
  E'en now, O Lord, relieve my woes;
Into Thy rest of love receive,
  And bless me with a calm repose.

E'en now my weary soul release,
  And raise me by Thy gracious hand;
Guide me into Thy perfect peace,
  And bring me to the promised land.

55. HARMONY GROVE. C. M.

Approach, my soul! the mercy seat,
  Where Jesus answers prayer;
There humbly fall before his feet,
  For none can perish there.

Thy promise is my only plea,
  With this I venture nigh:
Thou callest burdened souls to thee,
  And such, O Lord! am I.

Bow'd down beneath a load of sin,
  By Satan sorely pressed,
By wars without and fears within,
  I come to thee for rest.

Be thou my shield and hiding-place,
  That, sheltered near thy side,
I may my fierce accuser face,
  And tell him —"Thou hast died."

Oh! wondrous love,—to bleed and die,
  To bear the cross and shame,
That guilty sinners, such as I,
  Might plead thy gracious name!

56. AVON. C. M.

Mercy alone can meet my case,
  For mercy, Lord, I cry;
Jesus, Redeemer, show thy face
  In mercy, or I die.

Save me, for none beside can save;
  At thy command I tread,
With failing steps, life's stormy wave;
  The wave goes o'er my head.

I perish, and my doom were just;
  But wilt thou leave me?—No!
I hold thee fast, my hope, my trust;
  I will not let thee go.

To thee, thee only will I cleave;
  Thy word is all my plea;
That word is truth, and I believe—
  Have mercy, Lord, on me.

57.   OLMUTZ. S. M.

Oh, whither should I go,
  Burdened, and sick, and faint?
To whom should I my troubles show
  And pour out my complaint?

My Saviour bids me come,
  Ah, why do I delay?
He calls the weary sinner home,
  And yet from Him I stay.

What worldly tie must break,
  What idol yet depart,
Which will not let the Saviour take
  Possession of my heart?

Lord, break the fatal chain,
  And all my bonds remove;
Nor let one bosom sin remain
  To keep me from Thy love.

58.   WARD, OR ZEPHYR. L. M.

With tearful eyes I look around,
  Life seems a dark and stormy sea;

Yet, 'mid the gloom, I hear a sound,
  A heavenly whisper, "Come to me."

It tells me of a place of rest,
  It tells me where my soul may flee;
Oh! to the weary, faint, oppressed,
  How sweet the bidding, "Come to me!"

Oh voice of mercy! voice of love!
  In conflict, grief, and agony,
Support me, cheer me from above!
  And gently whispers, "Come to me."

I come; all else must fail and die,
  Earth has no resting-place for me;
To Christ I lift my weeping eye,
  Thou art my hope; I come to Thee.

59. BALERMA, EVAN, OR RISSAH. C. M.

PROSTRATE, dear Jesus, at Thy feet
  A guilty rebel lies,
And upwards to Thy mercy-seat
  Presumes to lift his eyes.

If tears of sorrow would suffice
  To pay the debt I owe,
Tears should from both my weeping eyes
  In ceaseless torrents flow.

But no such sacrifice I plead
  To expiate my guilt;

No tears but those which Thou hast shed,
  No blood, but Thou hast spilt.

Think of Thy sorrows, dearest Lord,
  And all my sins forgive;
Justice will well approve the word
  That bids the sinner live.

60.   AVON.   C. M.

O Thou, whose tender mercy hears
  Contrition's humble sigh,
Whose hand indulgent wipes the tears
  From sorrow's weeping eye,—

See, low before Thy throne of grace,
  A wretched wand'rer mourn;
Hast Thou not bid me seek Thy face?
  Hast Thou not said—Return?

And shall my guilty fears prevail
  To drive me from Thy feet?
O let not this dear refuge fail,
  This only safe retreat.

Absent from Thee, my Guide, my Light,
  Without one cheering ray,
Through dangers, fears, and gloomy night,
  How desolate my way.

O shine on this benighted heart,
   With beams of mercy shine;
And let Thy healing voice impart
   A taste of joys divine.

61.   HORTON. 7's.

Depth of mercy! can there be
Mercy still reserved for me?
Can my God his wrath forbear,
Me, the chief of sinners spare?

I have long withstood his grace,
Long provoked him to his face,
Would not hear his gracious calls
Grieved him by a thousand falls.

There for me the Saviour stands,
Shows his wounds and spreads his hands:
God is love! I know, I feel,
Jesus weeps and loves me still.

Lord, incline me to repent,
Let me now my fall lament,
Deeply my revolt deplore,
Weep, believe, and sin no more.

62.   "EVEN ME." P. M.

Lord, I hear the showers of blessing,
   Thou art scattering full and free—
Showers, the thirsty land refreshing;
   Let some droppings fall on me—Even me.

THE SINNER REPENTING.

Pass me not, O God, my Father!
  Sinful though my heart may be;
Thou might'st leave me, but the rather
  Let thy mercy light on me!—Even me.

Pass me not, O gracious Saviour!
  Let me live and cling to thee;
For I'm longing for thy favor;
  While thou'rt calling, call on me—Even me.

Pass me not, O mighty Spirit!
  Thou canst make the blind to see;
Witnesser of Jesus' merit!
  Speak some word of power to me—Even me.

Have I long in sin been sleeping—
  Long been slighting, grieving thee?
Has the world my heart been keeping?
  O forgive, and rescue me!—Even me.

Love of God—so pure and changeless;
  Blood of Christ—so rich and free;
Grace of God—so strong and boundless,
  Magnify it all in me!—Even me.

63.   WARD. L. M.

Show pity, Lord; O Lord, forgive,
Let a repenting rebel live;
Are not thy mercies large and free?
May not a sinner trust in thee?

My crimes are great, but don't surpass
The power and glory of thy grace;
Great God, thy nature hath no bound,
So let thy pardoning love be found.

O! wash my soul from every sin,
And make my guilty conscience clean;
Here on my heart the burden lies,
And past offences pain my eyes.

My lips with shame my sins confess,
Against thy law; against thy grace;
Lord, should thy judgment grow severe,
I am condemned, but thou art clear.

Should sudden vengeance seize my breath
I must pronounce thee just in death;
And if my soul were sent to hell,
Thy righteous law approves it well.

Yet, save a trembling sinner, Lord,
Whose hope, still hovering round thy word,
Would light on some sweet promise there,
Some sure support against despair.

64.   HORTON, 7's.

Jesus, save my dying soul,
Make the broken spirit whole,
Humble in the dust I lie,—
Saviour, leave me not to die.

Jesus, full of every grace,
Now reveal Thy smiling face;
Grant the joys of sin forgiv'n,
Foretaste of the bliss of heav'n.

All my guilt to Thee is known,
Thou art righteous, Thou alone;
All my help is from Thy cross,
All beside I count but loss.

Lord in Thee I now believe,
Wilt Thou, wilt Thou not forgive?
Helpless at Thy feet I lie,
Saviour, leave me not to die.

65. WARE (NEW.) L. M.

I WAS a traitor, doomed to die,
  Bound to endure eternal pains;
When Jesus saw me from on high,
  Was moved by love, and broke my chains.

Did melting pity stoop so low,
  The Lord of heaven pour out his blood,
To save our rebel-race from woe,
  And be our Advocate with God?

Infinite mercy! boundless love!
  Stand in amaze, ye rolling skies!
The Son of God, his grace to prove,
  Hangs on a tree, and groans, and dies!

66.   GANGES, C. P. M

Awaked by Sinai's awful sound,
My soul in bonds of guilt I found,
   And knew not where to go;
Eternal truth did loud proclaim,
"The sinner must be born again,
   Or sink to endless woe."

When to the law I trembling fled,
It poured its curses on my head,
   I no relief could find;
This fearful truth increased my pain,
"The sinner must be born again,"
   And whelmed my tortured mind.

Again did Sinai's thunder roll,
And guilt lay heavy on my soul,
   A vast oppressive load;
Alas, I read and saw it plain,
"The sinner must be born again,
   Or drink the wrath of God."

The saints I heard with rapture tell,
How Jesus conquered death and hell,
   And broke the fowler's snare;
Yet when I found this truth remain,
"The sinner must be born again,"
   I sunk in deep despair.

THE SINNER REPENTING.

But while I thus in anguish lay,
The gracious Saviour passed this way,
   And felt his pity move;
The sinner, by his justice slain,
Now by his grace is born again,
   And sings redeeming love.

67.   GANGES, C. P. M.

Lo! on a narrow neck of land,
'Twixt two unbounded seas I stand,
   Yet how insensible!
A point of time, a moment's space,
Removes me to yon heavenly place,
   Or shuts me up in hell.

O God, my inmost soul convert,
And deeply on my thoughtless heart,
   Eternal things impress;
Give me to feel their solemn weight,
And save me ere it be too late;
   Wake me to righteousness.

Before me place in bright array,
The pomp of that tremendous day,
   When thou with clouds shalt come
To judge the nations at thy bar;
And tell me, Lord, shall I be there,
   To meet a joyful doom?

Be this my one great business here,
With holy trembling, holy fear,
  To make my calling sure;
Thine utmost counsel to fulfil,
And suffer all thy righteous will,
  And to the end endure.

Then, Saviour, then my soul receive,
Transported from this vale, to live
  And reign with thee above;
Where faith is sweetly lost in sight,
And hope, in full, supreme delight,
  And everlasting love.

68.   KENTUCKY.   S. M.

And can I yet delay
  My little all to give?
To tear my soul from earth away,
  My Jesus to receive?

Nay, but I yield, I yield!
  I can hold out no more:
I sink, by dying love compelled,
  And own thee conqueror!

Though late, I all forsake,
  My friends, my all resign;
Gracious Redeemer, take, oh take,
  And seal me ever thine!

69. MISSIONARY HYMN, OR BEREA, 7, 6.

I lay my sins on Jesus,
    The spotless Lamb of God;
He bears them all, and frees us
    From the accursed load:
I bring my guilt to Jesus,
    To wash my crimson stains
White in His blood most precious,
    Till not a spot remains.

I lay my wants on Jesus,—
    All fulness dwells in Him;
He healeth my diseases,
    He doth my soul redeem;
I lay my griefs on Jesus,
    My burdens and my cares;
He from them all releases,
    He all my sorrows shares.

I long to be like Jesus,
    Meek, loving, lowly, mild;
I long to be like Jesus,
    The Father's holy child;
I long to be with Jesus
    Amid the heav'nly throng,
To sing with saints His praises,
    And learn the angels' song.

70. ELLIOT, OR HEBRON. L. M.

Just as I am, without one plea
But that Thy blood was shed for me,
And that Thou bid'st me come to Thee,
 O Lamb of God, I come.

Just as I am, and waiting not
To rid my soul of one dark blot,
To Thee, whose blood can cleanse each
 spot.
 O Lamb of God, I come.

Just as I am, though tossed about
With many a conflict, many a doubt,
Fightings within, and fears without,
 O Lamb of God, I come.

Just as I am, poor, wretched, blind,—
Sight, riches, healing of the mind,
Yea all I need in *Thee* to find,
 O Lamb of God, I come.

Just as I am, Thou wilt receive,
Wilt welcome, pardon, cleanse, relieve;
Because Thy promise I believe,
 O Lamb of God, I come.

71. AUTUMN, OR DORRANCE, 8, 7.

Take me, O my Father, take me,—
 Take me, save me, through Thy Son·

That which Thou wouldst have me, make me,
  Let Thy will in me be done.

Long from Thee my footsteps straying,
  Thorny proved the way I trod;
Weary come I now, and praying—
  Take me to Thy love, my God.

Fruitless years with grief recalling,
  Humbly I confess my sin;
At Thy feet, O Father, falling,
  To Thy household take me in.

Freely now to Thee I proffer
  This relenting heart of mine;
Freely, life and soul I offer,
  Gift unworthy love like Thine.

Once the world's Redeemer, dying,
  Bore our sins upon the tree;
On that sacrifice relying,
  Now I look in hope to Thee.

Father take me! all forgiving,
  Fold me to Thy loving breast;
In Thy love for ever living,
  I must be for ever blest.

72. ROCKBRIDGE, OR FOREST. L. M.

Here at thy cross, incarnate God,
I lay my soul beneath thy love;
Beneath the droppings of thy blood,
Jesus, nor shall it e'er remove.

Not all that tyrants think or say,
With rage and lightning in their eyes;
Nor hell shall fright my heart away,
Should hell with all its legions rise.

Should worlds conspire to drive me thence,
Moveless and firm this heart should lie;
Resolved, for that's my last defence,
If I must perish, there to die.

But speak, my Lord, and calm my fear;
Am I not safe beneath thy shade?
Thy vengeance will not strike me here,
Nor Satan dare my soul invade.

Yes, I'm secure beneath thy blood,
And all my foes shall lose their aim;
Hosanna to my Saviour God,
And my best honors to his name.

73. COMING TO JESUS.

Saviour, listen to our prayer,
Poor and sinful though we are;
   Guilt confessing, give thy blessing,
Grant thy loving care.

CHORUS.

O God our Father, Christ our King,
Now to thee our hearts we bring,
 Keep them ever, blessed Saviour,
Till in heaven thy love we sing.

Strength is thine; we often stray
From the pure and holy way;
 Wilt thou guide us, walk beside us,
Nearer every day?

Then may we, when life is o'er,
Stand with thee on yonder shore;
 Freed from sinning, heaven winning,
Praising evermore.

THE CONVERTED SINNER.

74.   HILLHURST. C. M. D.

I HEARD the voice of Jesus say,
 Come unto Me and rest,—
Lay down, thou weary one, lay down
 Thy head upon My breast:
I came to Jesus as I was,
 Weary, and worn, and sad;
I found in Him a resting-place,
 And He has made me glad

I heard the voice of Jesus say,
　I am this dark world's light,—
Look unto Me, thy morn shall rise,
　And all thy day be bright:
I looked to Jesus, and I found
　In Him my Star, my Sun;
And in that light of life I'll walk,
　Till travelling days are done.

75.   "I DO BELIEVE."

FATHER, I stretch my hands to thee;
　No other help I know;
If thou withdraw thyself from me,
　Ah, whither shall I go?

CHORUS.

　I do believe, I now believe
　　That Jesus died for me;
　And through his blood, his precious blood.
　　I shall from sin be free.

What did thine only son endure
　Before I drew my breath!
What pain, what labor to secure
　My soul from endless death?

Author of faith, to thee I lift
　My weary, longing eyes;
O may I now receive that gift;
　My soul, without it dies.

76. HILLHURST. C. M. D.

Jesus, Thou art the sinner's Friend,
  As such I look to Thee;
Now in the fulness of Thy love,
  O Lord, remember me:
Remember Thy pure word of grace,
  Remember Calvary,
Remember all Thy dying groans;
  And then remember me.

Thou Wondrous Advocate with God,
  I yield myself to Thee;
While Thou art sitting on Thy throne,
  Dear Lord, remember me;
Lord, I am guilty, I am vile,
  But Thy salvation's free;
Then, in Thine all-abounding grace,
  Dear Lord, remember me.

Howe'er forsaken or distressed,
  Howe'er oppressed I be,
Howe'er afflicted here on earth,
  Do Thou remember me:
And when I close my eyes in death,
  When creature-helps all flee,
Then, O my dear Redeemer, God,
  I pray remember me.

77. WARE. (NEW.) L. M.

Jesus, my all, to heaven is gone,
He, whom I fixed my hopes upon;
His track I see, and I'll pursue
The narrow way, till him I view.

The way the holy prophets went,
The road that leads from banishment,
The King's highway of holiness
I'll go, for all his paths are peace.

This is the way I long have sought,
And mourned because I found it not;
My grief and burden long have been,
Because I could not cease from sin.

The more I strove against its power,
I sinned and stumbled but the more,
Till late I heard my Saviour say,
"Come hither, soul, I am the way."

Lo! glad I come, and thou, blest Lamb,
Shall take me to thee as I am:
Nothing but sin I thee can give,
Nothing but love shall I receive.

78. ROLLAND. L. M.

Oh happy day, that fixed my choice
  On Thee, my Saviour, and my God!

Well may this glowing heart rejoice,
  And tell its raptures all abroad.

Oh, happy bond, that seals my vows
  To Him who merits all my love ;
Let cheerful anthems fill His house,
  While to that sacred shrine I move.

'Tis done, the great transaction's done,
  I am my Lord's, and He is mine :
He drew me, and I followed on,
  Charmed to confess the voice divine.

High heaven, that heard the solemn vow,
  That vow renewed sha'l daily hear ;
Till in life's latest hour I bow,
  And bless in death a bond so dear.

79. AMAZING GRACE. C. M.

Amazing grace! how sweet the sound,
  That saved a wretch like me !
I once was lost, but now am found,
  Was blind, but now I see.

'Twas grace that taught my heart to fear,
  And grace my fears relieved :
How precious did that grace appear,
  The hour I first believed !

Through many dangers, toils and snares,
  I have already come ;

'Tis grace that brought me safe thus far,
  And grace will lead me home.

The Lord has promised good to me,
  His word my hope secures;
He will my shield and portion be,
  As long as life endures.

And when this flesh and heart shall fail,
  And mortal life shall cease;
I shall possess, within the veil,
  A life of joy and peace.

80.   THE CONVERT. 6's, 9's.

  How happy are they
  Who the Saviour obey,
And have laid up their treasures above!
  O what tongue can express
  The sweet comfort and peace
Of a soul in its earliest love?

  'Twas heaven below
  My Redeemer to know,
And the angels could do nothing more,
  Than to fall at his feet,
  And the story repeat,
And the lover of sinners adore.

  O the rapturous height
  Of that holy delight,

Which I felt in the life giving blood!
   Of my Saviour possessed,
   I was perfectly blest,
As if filled with the fulness of God.

   Then, all the day long,
   Was my Jesus my song,
And redemption through faith in his name;
   O that all might believe,
   And salvation receive,
And their song and their joy be the same.

81.   GANGES. C. P. M.

O THOU that hear'st the prayer of faith;
Wilt thou not save a soul from death,
   That casts itself on thee?
I have no refuge of my own,
But fly to what my Lord has done
   And suffered once for me.

Slain in the guilty sinner's stead,
His spotless righteousness I plead,
   And his atoning blood:
Thy righteousness my robe shall be,
Thy merit shall avail for me,
   And bring me near to God.

Then snatch me from eternal death,
The spirit of adoption breathe,
   His consolation send:

By him some word of life impart,
And sweetly whisper to my heart,
 "Thy Maker is thy Friend."

The king of terrors then would be
A welcome messenger to me,
 To bid me come away:
Unclogged by earth, or earthly things,
I'd mount, I'd fly with eager wings,
 To everlasting day.

82.   MARTYN. 7's DOUBLE.

People of the living God,
I have sought the world around,
Paths of sin and sorrow trod,
Peace and comfort no where found:
Now to you my spirit turns,
Turns a fugitive unblest;
Brethren, where your altar burns,
O! receive me into rest.

Lonely, I no longer roam,
Like the cloud, the wind, the wave;
Where you dwell shall be my home,
Where you die shall be my grave:
Mine the God whom you adore,
Your Redeemer shall be mine,
Earth can fill my soul no more,
Every idol I resign.

Tell me not of gain or loss,
Ease, enjoyment, pomp or power,
Welcome poverty and cross.
Shame, reproach, affliction's hour:
" Follow me:" I know thy voice;
Jesus, Lord, thy steps I see;
Now I take thy yoke, by choice;
Light thy burden now to me.

83. BALERMA, OR AZMON. C. M.

How sad our state by nature is!
   Our sin how deep it stains!
And Satan binds our captive minds
   Fast in his slavish chains.

But there's a voice of sovereign grace
   Sounds from the sacred word:
"Ho! ye despairing sinners, come,
   And trust upon the Lord."

My soul obeys the almighty call,
   And runs to this relief:
I would believe thy promise, Lord,
   O help my unbelief.

To the dear fountain of thy blood,
   Incarnate God, I fly:
Here let me wash my spotted soul,
   From crimes of deepest die.

Stretch out thine arm, victorious King,
   My reigning sins subdue;
Drive the old dragon from his seat,
   With all his hellish crew.

A guilty, weak and helpless worm,
   On thy kind arms I fall:
Be thou my strength and righteousness,
   My Jesus and my all.

84.   EVAN. C. M.

I'm not ashamed to own my Lord,
   Nor to defend his cause,
Maintain the honor of his word,
   The glory of his cross.

Jesus, my God, I know his name,
   His name is all my trust;
Nor will he put my soul to shame,
   Nor let my hope be lost.

Firm as his throne his promise stands,
   And he can well secure
What I've committed to his hands,
   Till the decisive hour.

Then will he own my worthless name,
   Before his Father's face,
And in the new Jerusalem,
   Appoint my soul a place.

85.   HEBRON. L. M.

Jesus, and shall it ever be,
A mortal man ashamed of thee?
Ashamed of thee, whom angels praise,
Whose glories shine through endless days!

Ashamed of Jesus! sooner far
Let evening blush to own a star;
He sheds the beams of light divine,
O'er this benighted soul of mine.

Ashamed of Jesus! just as soon
Let midnight be ashamed of noon;
'Tis midnight with my soul, till he,
Bright Morning Star, bid darkness flee.

Ashamed of Jesus! that dear friend
On whom my hopes of heaven depend!
No, when I blush, be this my shame.
That I no more revere his name.

Ashamed of Jesus! Yes I may,
When I've no guilt to wash away,
No tear to wipe, no good to crave,
No fears to quell, no soul to save.

Till then—nor is my boasting vain—
Till then, I boast a Saviour slain:
And O may this my glory be,
That Christ is not ashamed of me.

CHRISTIAN EXPERIENCE.

86. ROCKINGHAM. L. M.

Ah wretched souls who strive in vain,
Slaves to the world, and slaves to sin;
A nobler toil may I sustain,
A nobler satisfaction win.

May I resolve with all my heart,
With all my powers to serve the Lord;
Nor from his precepts e'er depart,
Whose service is a rich reward.

O! be his service all my joy!
Around let my example shine,
'Till others love the blest employ,
And join in labors so divine.

Be this the purpose of my soul,
My solemn, my determined choice,
To yield to his supreme control,
And in his kind commands rejoice.

O! may I never faint nor tire,
Nor wandering leave his sacred ways:
Great God, accept my soul's desire,
And give me strength to live thy praise.

87. ROCKINGHAM OR DUNLAP'S CREEK.
C. M.

When, rising from the bed of death,
   O'erwhelmed with guilt and fear,
I see my Maker face to face,
   O how shall I appear?

If yet while pardon may be found,
   And mercy may be sought,
My heart with inward horror shrinks,
   And trembles at the thought;

When thou, O Lord, shalt stand disclosed,
   In majesty severe,
And sit in judgment on my soul,
   O how shall I appear?

Yet never shall my soul despair
   Her pardon to procure,
Who knows thine only son has died,
   To make her pardon sure.

88. CONWAY. C. M.

Come, let us join our cheerful songs,
   With angels round the throne;
Ten thousand thousand are their tongues,
   But all their joys are one.

"Worthy the Lamb that died," they cry,
  "To be exalted thus,"
"Worthy the Lamb," our lips reply,
  "For he was slain for us."

Let all that dwell above the sky,
  And air, and earth, and seas,
Conspire to lift thy glories high,
  And speak thine endless praise.

The whole creation join in one,
  To bless the sacred name
Of Him who sits upon the throne,
  And to adore the lamb.

89.   EVAN, OR ORTONVILLE. C. M.

O! for a closer walk with God,
  A calm and heavenly frame;
A light to shine upon the road
  That leads me to the Lamb.

Where is the blessedness I knew
  When first I saw the Lord?
Where is the soul-refreshing view
  Of Jesus and his word?

What peaceful hours I once enjoyed,
  How sweet their memory still!
But they have left an aching void,
  The world can never fill.

Return, O holy Dove, return,
  Sweet messenger of rest;
I hate the sins that made thee mourn,
  And drove thee from my breast.

The dearest idol I have known,
  What e'er that idol be,
Help me to tear it from thy throne,
  And worship only thee.

90.   ELLIOT. 8, 6.

My God, my Father, while I stray
Far from my home, on life's rough way,
Oh teach me from my heart to say,
  "Thy will, O Lord, be done!"

If but my fainting heart be blest
With Thy sweet Spirit for its guest,
My God, to Thee I leave the rest;
  "Thy will, O Lord, be done!"

Renew my will from day to day;
Blend it with Thine, and take away

What e'er now makes it hard to say,
  "Thy will, O Lord, be done!"

91.   HERMON. C. M.

Come, let us join our friends above,
  That have obtained the prize;
And on the eagle wings of love,
  To joy celestial rise.

Let saints below his praises sing,
  With those to glory gone;
For all the servants of our King,
  In heaven and earth, are one.

One family, we dwell in him,
  One church above, beneath;
Though now divided by the stream
  The narrow stream of death.

One army of the living God,
  To his commands we bow;
Part of the host have crossed the flood,
  And part are crossing now.

92. NO SORROW THERE. C. M., OR
    ST. THOMAS.

Blest be the tie that binds
  Our hearts in Christian love;
The fellowship of kindred minds,
  Is like to that above.

Before our Father's throne
  We pour our ardent prayers:
Our fears, our hopes, our aims are one,
  Our comforts and our cares.

We share our mutual woes,
  Our mutual burdens bear,
And often for each other flows
  The sympathizing tear.

When we asunder part,
  It gives us inward pain;
But we shall still be joined in heart,
  And hope to meet again.

This glorious hope revives
  Our courage by the way;
While each in expectation lives,
  And longs to see the day,

From sorrow, toil, and pain,
  And sin we shall be free;
And perfect love and friendship reign,
  Through all eternity.

93.   AVON. C. M.

How oft, alas! this wretched heart
  Has wandered from the Lord!
How oft my roving thoughts depart,
  Forgetful of his word!

Yet sovereign mercy calls, "Return,"
  Dear Lord, and may I come?
My vile ingratitude I mourn:
  O take the wanderer home.

And canst thou, wilt thou, yet forgive,
  And bid my crimes remove?
And shall a pardoned rebel live
  To speak thy wondrous love?

Almighty grace, thy healing power,
  How glorious, how divine!
That can to life and bliss restore
  So vile a heart as mine.

Thy pardoning love, so free, so sweet,
  Dear Saviour, I adore;
O keep me at thy sacred feet,
  And let me rove no more.

94. CHRISTMAS, ZERAH, OR MAITLAND. C. M.

AM I a soldier of the cross,
  A follower of the Lamb,
And shall I fear to own his cause,
  Or blush to speak his name?

Must I be carried to the skies,
  On flowery beds of ease;
While others fought to win the prize,
  And sailed through bloody seas?

Are there no foes for me to face?
　Must I not stem the flood?
Is this dark world a friend to grace,
　To help me on to God?

Sure I must fight, if I would reign;
　Increase my courage, Lord;
I'll bear the toil, endure the pain,
　Supported by thy word.

95.   REDEEMING LOVE.   7's.

Come, my soul, thy suit prepare,
Jesus loves to answer prayer;
He himself has bid thee pray,
Therefore will not say thee nay.

Thou art coming to a King,
Large petitions with thee bring;
For his grace and power are such,
None can ever ask too much.

With my burden I begin,
Lord, remove this load of sin;
Let thy blood, for sinners spilt,
Set my conscience free from guilt.

Lord, I come to thee for rest,
Take possession of my breast;
There thy blood-bought right maintain,
And without a rival reign.

96. GOLDEN HILL. S. M.

Jesus, who knows full well
   The heart of every saint;
Invites us all our griefs to tell,
   To pray and never faint.

He bows his gracious ear,
   We never plead in vain:
Yet we must wait till he appear,
   And pray, and pray again.

Though unbelief suggest,
   Why should we longer wait?
He bids us never give him rest,
   But be importunate.

Jesus the Lord will hear
   His chosen when they cry,
Yes, though he may a while forbear,
   He'll help them from on high.

97. LABAN. S. M.

My soul, be on thy guard,
   Ten thousand foes arise;
And hosts of sins are pressing hard,
   To draw thee from the skies.

O watch, and fight, and pray,
   The battle ne'er give o'er;

Renew it boldly every day,
  And help divine implore.

Ne'er think the victory won,
  Nor once at ease sit down;
Thy arduous work will not be done,
  'Till thou hast got the crown.

Fight on, my soul, till death
  Shall bring thee to thy God;
He'll take thee, at thy parting breath,
  Up to his blest abode.

98. REDEEMING LOVE. 7'S. OR WESLEY.

I was a wand'ring sheep,
  I did not love the fold,
I did not love my Shepherd's voice,
  I would not be controlled;
I was a wayward child,
  I did not love my home,
I did not love my Father's voice,
  I loved afar to roam.

The Shepherd sought His sheep,
  The Father sought His child,
He followed me o'er vale and hill,
  O'er deserts waste and wild;
He found me nigh to death,
  Famished, faint, and lone;
He bound me with the bands of love,
  He saved the wand'ring one.

Jesus my Shepherd is,
  'Twas He that loved my soul,
Twas He that washed me in His blood,
  'Twas He that made me whole;
'Twas He that sought the lost,
  That found the wand'ring sheep,
Twas He that brought me to the fold,—
  'Tis He that still doth keep.

No more a wand'ring sheep,
  I love to be controlled,
I love my tender Shepherd's voice,
  I love the peaceful fold;
No more a wayward child,
  I seek no more to roam,
I love my heav'nly Father's voice,—
  I love, I love His home.

99.   REDEEMING LOVE.   7's.

'Tis a point I long to know,
  Oft it causes anxious thought;
Do I love the Lord, or no?
  Am I his, or am I not?

If I love, why am I thus?
  Why this dull and lifeless frame?
Hardly, sure, can they be worse,
  Who have never heard his name?

Could my heart so hard remain,
  Prayer a task and burden prove,

Every trifle give me pain,
  If I knew a Saviour's love?

When I turn my eyes within,
  All is dark, and vain, and wild:
Filled with unbelief and sin,
  Can I deem myself a child?

If I pray, or hear, or read,
  Sin is mixed with all I do;
You who love the Lord indeed,
  Tell me—is it thus with you?

Yet I mourn my stubborn will,
  Find my sin a grief and thrall;
Should I grieve for what I feel,
  If I did not love at all?

Lord, decide the doubtful case,
  Thou who art thy people's Sun:
Shine upon thy work of grace,
  If it be indeed begun.

100.   AUTUMN. 8, 7, D.

HOLY Father, Thou hast taught us
  We should live to Thee alone;
Year by year, Thy hand hath brought us,
  On through dangers oft unknown.
When we wandered, Thou hast found us,—
  When we doubted, sent us light;

Still Thine arm has been around us,
   All our paths were in Thy sight.

In the world will foes assail us,
   Craftier, stronger far than we;
And the strife shall never fail us
   Well we know, before we die.
Therefore, Lord, we come believing
   Thou canst give the pow'r we need,
Through the pray'r of faith receiving
   Strength, the Spirit's strength, indeed.

We would trust in Thy protecting,
   Wholly rest upon Thine arm;
Follow wholly Thy directing,
   Thou our only guard from harm;
Keep us from our own undoing,
   Help us turn to Thee when tried;
Still our footsteps, Father, viewing,
   Keep us ever at Thy side.

101.   CROSS AND CROWN.   C. M.

Must Jesus bear the cross alone,
   And all the world go free?
No, there's a cross for every one,
   And there's a cross for me.

The consecrated cross I'll bear,
   Till death shall set me free;

And then go home my crown to wear,
  For there's a crown for me.

Before the great, the heavenly throne,
  And Jesus' pierced feet,
Joyful I'll cast my golden crown,
  And His dear name repeat.

O precious cross! O glorious crown!
  O resurrection day!
Let angels from Thy throne come down,
  And bear my soul away.

102.   DORRANCE. 8, 7.

  Sweet the moments, rich in blessing,
    Which before the cross I spend,
  Life, and health, and peace possessing,
    From the sinner's dying Friend.

  Here I'll sit for ever viewing
    Mercy stream in streams of blood;
  Precious drops, my soul bedewing,
    Plead and claim my peace with God.

  Truly blessed is this station,
    Low before his cross to lie;
  While I see divine compassion
    Floating in his languid eye.

  Here it is I find my heaven,
    While upon the cross I gaze;

Love I much? I'm much forgiven,
　I'm a miracle of grace.

Love and grief my heart dividing,
　With my tears, his feet I bathe;
Constant still in faith abiding,
　Life deriving from his death.

103. SWANWICK, OR CHRISTMAS. C. M.

To our Redeemer's glorious name
　Awake the sacred song;
O may His love—immortal flame—
　Tune every heart and tongue.

For us He left His throne on high,
　Left the bright realms of bliss,
And came on earth to bleed and die—
　Was ever love like this?

Dear Lord, while we adoring pay
　Our humble thanks to Thee,
May every heart with rapture say,—
　"The Saviour died for me."

O may the sweet, the blissful theme
　Fill every heart and tongue,
Till strangers love Thy charming name,
　And join the sacred song.

104. LOVING-KINDNESS. L. M.

Awake, my soul, in joyful lays,
And sing my great Redeemer's praise,
He justly claims a song from thee;
His loving kindness, O! how free.

He saw me ruined in the fall,
Yet loved me, notwithstanding all;
He saved me from my lost estate;
His loving kindness, O! how great!

Though numerous hosts of mighty foes,
Though earth and hell my way oppose,
He safely leads my soul along;
His loving kindness, O! how strong!

When trouble, like a gloomy cloud,
Has gathered thick, and thundered loud,
He near my soul has always stood;
His loving kindness, O! how good!

Often I feel my sinful heart
Prone from my Saviour to depart;
But though I oft have him forgot,
His loving kindness changes not.

Soon shall I pass the gloomy vale,
Soon all my mortal powers must fail;
O, may my last expiring breath,
His loving kindness sing in death.

105.   CHRISTMAS.   C. M.

Awake, my soul, stretch every nerve,
  And press with vigor on;
A heavenly race demands thy zeal,
  And an immortal crown.

A cloud of witnesses around
  Hold thee in full survey;
Forget the steps already trod,
  And onward urge thy way.

'Tis God's all animating voice,
  That calls thee from on high;
'Tis his own hand presents the prize
  To thine aspiring eye.

Blest Saviour, introduced by thee,
  Have I my race begun;
And, crowned with victory, at thy feet
  I'll lay my honors down.

106.   REDEEMING LOVE.   7's.

Now begin the heavenly theme,
Sing aloud in Jesus' name;
Ye, who his salvation prove,
Triumph in redeeming love.

Ye, who see the Father's grace
Beaming in the Saviour's face,

As to Canaan on ye move,
Praise and bless redeeming love.

Mourning souls, dry up your tears;
Banish all your guilty fears;
See your guilt and curse remove,
Cancelled by redeeming love.

Ye, alas! who long have been
Willing slaves to death and sin,
Now from bliss no longer rove,
Stop and taste redeeming love.

Welcome all, by sin oppressed,
Welcome to his sacred rest;
Nothing brought him from above,
Nothing but redeeming love.

107. BEZA. 7, 6, 8,

LAMB of God! whose bleeding love
  We now recall to mind,
Send the answer from above,
  And let us mercy find;
Think on us who think on Thee,
  And ev'ry burdened soul release;
Oh remember Calvary,
  And bid us go in peace.

By Thine agonizing pain
  And bloody sweat, we pray,—

By Thy dying love to man,
  Take all our sins away;
Burst our bonds, and set us free,
  From all iniquity release;
Oh remember Calvary,
  And bid us go in peace.

Let Thy blood, by faith applied,
  The sinner's pardon seal,
Own us freely justified,
  And all our sickness heal:
By Thy passion on the tree,
  Let all our griefs and troubles cease
Oh remember Calvary,
  And bid us go in peace.

108.   AUTUMN.   7, 8. D.

Jesus, I my cross have taken,
  All to leave and follow thee;
Naked, poor, despised, forsaken,
  Thou from hence my All shall be;
Let the world neglect and leave me;
  They have left my Saviour too;
Human hopes have oft deceived me;
  Thou art faithful, thou art true.

Perish, earthly fame and treasure,
  Come disaster, scorn, and pain;
In thy service, pain is pleasure;
  With thy favor, loss is gain:

O 'tis not in grief to harm me,
  While thy bleeding love I see;
O 'tis not in joy to charm me,
  When that love is hid from me.

109. NOTTINGHILL. C. M.

My God! my Father! blissful name!
  Oh! may I call thee mine?
May I with sweet assurance claim
  A portion so divine?

This only can my fears control,
  And bid my sorrows fly;
What harm can ever reach my soul
  Beneath my Father's eye?

What e'er thy providence denies,
  I calmly would resign;
For thou art good and just, and wise,
  Oh! bend my will to thine.

What e'r thy sacred will ordains,
  Oh! give me strength to bear;
Let me but know my Father reigns,
  And trust his tender care.

110. HERMON, OR NOTTINGHILL. C. M.

O! how I love thy holy law!
  'Tis daily my delight:

And thence my meditations draw
  Divine advice by night.

My waking eyes prevent the day
  To meditate thy word :
My soul with longing melts away,
  To hear thy gospel, Lord.

Thy heavenly words my heart engage,
  And well employ my tongue,
And in my tiresome pilgrimage
  Yield me a heavenly song.

Am I a stranger, or at home,
  'Tis my perpetual feast ;
Not honey dropping from the comb
  So much allures the taste.

No treasures so enrich the mind ;
  Nor shall thy word be sold
For loads of silver well refined,
  Nor heaps of choicest gold.

When nature sinks, and spirits droop,
  Thy promises of grace
Are pillars to support my hope;
  And there I write thy praise.

111.   JESUS IS MINE.

  FADE, fade each earthly joy,
    Jesus is mine;

Break every tender tie,
  Jesus is mine;
Dark is the wilderness,
Earth has no resting-place,
Jesus alone can bless,
  Jesus is mine.

Tempt not my soul away,
  Jesus is mine;
Here would I ever stay,
  Jesus is mine;
Perishing things of clay,
Born but for one brief day,
Pass from my heart away,
  Jesus is mine.

Farewell, ye dreams of night,
  Jesus is mine;
Lost in the dawning light,
  Jesus is mine;
All that my soul has tried,
Left but a dismal void,
Jesus has satisfied,
  Jesus is mine.

Farewell mortality,
  Jesus is mine;
Welcome eternity,
  Jesus is mine;
Welcome, O loved and blest,
Welcome, sweet scenes of rest,

Welcome my Saviour's breast,
  Jesus is mine.

112.   GIVE.   C. M.

The Lord's my Shepherd, I'll not want,
  He makes me down to lie
In pastures green: he leadeth me
  The quiet waters by.

My soul he doth restore again,
  And me to walk doth make
Within the paths of righteousness,
  Even for his own name's sake.

Yea, though I walk in death's dark vale
  Yet will I fear no ill;
For thou art with me, and thy rod
  And staff me comfort still.

My table thou hast furnished
  In presence of my foes;
My head thou dost with oil anoint,
  And my cup overflows.

Goodness and mercy all my life,
  Shall surely follow me:
And in God's house forevermore
  My dwelling place shall be.

113. NAOMI. C. M.

My times of sorrow and of joy,
  Great God are in thy hand;
All my enjoyments come from thee,
  And go at thy command.

O Lord shouldst thou withhold them all,
  Yet would I not repine:
Before they were by me possessed,
  They were entirely thine.

Nor would I drop a murmuring word,
  If all the world were gone,
But seek substantial happiness,
  In thee and thee alone.

114. NAOMI, OR NOTTINGHILL. C. M.

O God of Bethel, by whose hand
  Thy people still are fed;
Who through this weary pilgrimage,
  Hast all our fathers led;

Our vows, our prayers, we now present
  Before thy throne of grace:
God of our fathers be the God
  Of their succeeding race.

Through each perplexing path of life,
  Our wandering footsteps guide;

Give us each day our daily bread,
   And raiment fit provide.

O spread thy covering wings around,
   Till all our wanderings cease,
And at our Father's loved abode
   Our souls arrive in peace.

Such blessings from thy gracious hand
   Our humble prayers implore;
And thou shalt be our chosen God,
   And portion evermore.

115.   ROSEBANK. 8, 7, 4.

SAVIOUR, like a shepherd lead us;
   Much we need thy tender care;
In thy pleasant pastures feed us;
   For our use thy folds prepare:
||: Blssed! Jesus Blessed Jesus!
   Thou hast bought us, thine we are. :||

Thou hast promised to receive us,
   Poor and sinful though we be;
Thou hast mercy to relieve us,
   Grace to cleanse, and power to free:
Blessed Jesus! Blessed Jesus!
   Let us early turn to thee.

Early let us seek thy favor;
   Early let us learn thy will;
Do thou, Lord, our only Saviour,

With thy love our bosoms fill;
  Blessed Jesus! Blessed Jesus!
  Thou hast loved us,—love us still.

116.　　　FOUNT.　8, 7, D.

COME, Thou Fount of every blessing,
  Tune my heart to sing Thy grace;
Streams of mercy never ceasing,
  Call for songs of loudest praise;
Teach me some melodious sonnet,
  Sung by flaming tongues above;
Praise the mount,—O fix me on it,—
  Mount of God's unchanging love.

Here I raise my Ebenezer,
  Hither by Thy help I'm come;
And I hope, by Thy good pleasure,
  Safely to arrive at home;
Jesus sought me when a stranger,
  Wand'ring from the fold of God;
He, to rescue me from danger,
  Interposed with precious blood.

Oh to grace how great a debtor,
  Daily I'm constrained to be!
Let that grace, Lord, like a fetter,
  Bind my wand'ring heart to Thee:
Prone to wander, Lord, I feel it,
  Prone to leave the God I love;
Here's my heart, Lord, take and seal it,—
  Seal it from thy courts above,

117. AUTUMN. 8, 7, D.

Gently, Lord, O! gently lead us,
  Through this lonely vale of tears;
Through the changes thou 'st decreed us,
  Till our last great change appears.
When Temptation's darts assail us,
  When in devious paths we stray,
Let thy goodness never fail us,
  Lead us in thy perfect way.

In the hour of pain and anguish,
  In the hour when death draws near,
Suffer not our hearts to languish,
  Suffer not our souls to fear,
And when mortal life is ended,
  Bid us in thine arms to rest,
Till by angel bands attended,
  We awake among the blest.

EVENING.

118. BROWN, OR MARLOW. C. M.

I love to steal awhile away
  From every cumbering care;
And spend the hours of setting day,
  In humble, grateful prayer.

I love in solitude to shed
  The penitential tear,

And all his promises to plead,
  Where none but God can hear.

I love to think on mercies past,
  And future good implore,
And all my cares and sorrows cast
  On him whom I adore.

I love by faith to take a view
  Of brighter scenes in heaven;
The prospect does my strength renew,
  While here by tempests driven.

Thus, when life's toilsome day is o'er,
  May its departing ray
Be calm as this impressive hour,
  And lead to endless day.

119.   GIVE.   C. M.

DREAD Sov'reign let my evening song
  Like holy incense rise;
Assist the off'rings of my tongue
  To reach the lofty skies.

Through all the dangers of the day
  Thy hand was still my guard;
And still to drive my wants away
  Thy mercy stood prepared.

Perpetual blessings from above
  Encompassed me around;

But oh how few returns of love
  Has my Creator found!

What have I done for Him who died
  To save my wretched soul?
How are my follies multiplied,
  Fast as my minutes roll!

Lord, with this guilty heart of mine
  To Thy dear cross I flee,
And to Thy grace my soul resign,
  To be renewed by Thee.

120.   AUTUMN, OR ERITH.   8, 7.

SAVIOUR, breathe an evening blessing,
  Ere repose our spirits seal:
Sin and want we come confessing,
  Thou canst save and thou canst heal.
Though destruction walk around us,
  Though the arrow near us fly,
Angel-guards from thee surround us,
  We are safe if thou art nigh.

Though the night be dark and dreary,
  Darkness cannot hide from thee;
Thou art he who, never weary,
  Watchest where thy people be.
Should swift death this night o'ertake us,
  And our couch become our tomb,
May the morn, in heaven awake us,
  Clad in light and deathless bloom.

MISSIONARY

121. HARWELL. 8, 7, DOUBLE, OR TELLEMANN

Sion's King shall reign victorious,
  All the earth shall own his sway;
He will make his kingdom glorious,
  He shall reign through endless day.

Nations, now from God estranged,
  Then shall see a glorious light;
Night to day shall then be changed,
  Heaven shall triumph in the sight.

See the ancient idols falling,
  Worshipped once, but now abhorred,
Men on Sion's King are calling,
  Sion's King by all adored.

Then shall Israel long dispersed,
  Mourning seek their Lord and God,
Look on him whom once they pierced,
  Own and kiss the chastening rod.

Then shall Israel all be saved,
  War and tumult then shall cease,
While the greater Son of David
  Rules a conquered world in peace.

Mighty King, thine arm revealing,
  Now thy glorious cause maintain;

Bring the nations help and healing,
 Make them subject to thy reign!

122. HARWELL. 8, 7, DOUBLE.

Glorious things of thee are spoken,
 Sion, city of our God;
He whose word cannot be broken,
 Formed thee for his own abode:
On the rock of ages founded,
 What can shake thy sure repose?
With Salvation's walls surrounded,
 Thou mayst smile at all thy foes.

See the streams of living waters,
 Springing from eternal love,
Well supply thy sons and daughters,
 And all fear of want remove.
Who can faint while such a river
 Ever flows their thirst to assuage;
Grace, which like the Lord, the giver,
 Never fails from age to age?

Round each habitation hovering,
 See the cloud and fire appear,
For a glory and a covering,
 Showing that the Lord is near:
Thus deriving from their banner,
 Light by night, and shade by day;
Safe they feed upon the manna,
 Which he gives them, when they pray.

123.   MISSIONARY HYMN.   7, 6.

From Greenland's icy mountains,
　From India's coral strand,
Where Afric's sunny fountains
　Roll down their golden sand,
From many an ancient river,
　From many a palmy plain,
They call us to deliver
　Their land from error's chain.

What though the spicy breezes
　Blow soft o'er Ceylon's isle,
Though every prospect pleases,
　And only man is vile;
In vain with lavish kindness
　The gifts of God are strown,
The heathen, in their blindness,
　Bow down to wood and stone.

Shall we, whose souls are lighted,
　With wisdom from on high,
Shall we, to men benighted,
　The lamp of life deny?
Salvation, O salvation!
　The joyful sound proclaim,
Till earth's remotest nation
　Has learned Messiah's name.

124.   MISSIONARY HYMN.   7, 6.

HAIL to the Lord's Anointed!
  Great David's greater Son!
Hail in the time appointed,
  Thy reign on earth begun!
Thou com'st to break oppression,
  To set the captive free,
To take away transgression,
  And rule in equity.

Kings shall fall down before Thee
  And gold and incense bring,
All nations shall adore Thee,
  Thy praise all people sing;
For Thou shalt have dominion
  O'er river, sea, and shore,
Far as the eagle's pinion
  Or dove's light wing can soar.

O'er every foe victorious
  Thou on Thy throne shall rest,
From age to age more glorious,
  All-blessing and all-blest;
The tide of time shall never
  Thy covenant remove;
Thy name shall stand for ever,
  That name to us is LOVE.

125.   ANVERN, OR MIGDOL. L. M.

Soon may the last glad song arise
Through all the millions of the skies—
That song of triumph which records
That all the earth is now the Lord's!

Let thrones and powers and kingdoms be
Obedient, mighty God, to thee!
And, over land, and stream, and main,
Wave thou the sceptre of thy reign!

O let that glorious anthem swell,
Let host to host the triumph tell,
That not one rebel heart remains,
But over all the Saviour reigns!

126.   ANVERN. L. M.

Triumphant Zion! lift thy head
From dust, and darkness, and the dead!
Though humbled long—awake at length,
And gird thee with thy Saviour's strength.

Put all thy beauteous garments on,
And let thy excellence be known:
Decked in the robes of righteousness,
The world thy glories shall confess.

No more shall foes unclean invade,
And fill thy hallowed walls with dread:

No more shall hell's insulting host
Their victory and thy sorrows boast.

God, from on high, has heard thy prayer;
His hand thy ruins shall repair:
Nor will thy watchful Monarch cease
To guard thee in eternal peace

127.   MISSIONARY HYMN. 7, 6.

Now be the gospel banner
  In every land unfurled;
And be the shout, hosanna!
  Re-echoed through the world;
Till every isle and nation,
  Till every tribe and tongue,
Receive the great salvation,
  And join the happy throng.

What though the embattled legions
  Of earth and hell combine!
His arm throughout their regions,
  Shall soon resplendent shine:
Ride on, O Lord, victorious;
  Immanuel, Prince of peace,
Thy triumph shall be glorious!
  Thy empire still increase.

Yes, thou shalt reign for ever,
  O Jesus, King of kings;

Thy light, thy love, thy favor,
   Each ransomed captive sings;
The isles for thee are waiting,
   The deserts learn thy praise;
The hills and valleys greeting,
   The song responsive raise.

DEATH.

128.   OLMUTZ. S. M.

O! for the death of those
   Who slumber in the Lord!
O be, like theirs, my last repose,
   Like theirs my last reward!

Their bodies in the ground
   In silent hope may lie,
Till the last trumpet's joyful sound
   Shall call them to the sky.

Their ransomed spirits soar,
   On wings of faith and love,
To meet the Saviour they adore,
   And reign with him above.

With us their names shall live
   Through long succeeding years,
Embalmed with all our hearts can give,
   Our praises and our tears.

O for the death of those
  Who slumber in the Lord!
O be, like theirs, my last repose,
  Like theirs my last reward!

129. NAOMI. C. M.

Hear what the voice from heaven proclaims
  For all the pious dead;
Sweet is the savor of their names,
  And soft their sleeping bed.

They die in Jesus, and are blest;
  How calm their slumbers are!
From sufferings and from sin released,
  And freed from every snare.

Far from this world of toil and strife,
  They're present with the Lord;
The labors of their mortal life
  End in a large reward.

130. HAMBURG, OR REST. L. M.

Unveil thy bosom, faithful tomb,
Take this new treasure to thy trust,
And give these sacred relics room,
To slumber in the silent dust.

Nor pain, nor grief, nor anxious fear
Invades thy bounds—no mortal woes

Can reach the peaceful sleeper here,
While angels watch his soft repose.

So Jesus slept, God's dying Son
Passed through the grave, and blessed the bed;
Rest here, blest saint, till from his throne
The morning break, and pierce the shade.

Break from his throne, illustrious morn,
Attend, O earth, his sovereign word;
Restore thy trust—a glorious form
Shall then arise to meet the Lord.

131.   ZEPHYR.   L. M.

How blest the righteous when he dies!
When sinks a weary soul to rest,
How mildly beam the closing eyes,
How gently heaves the expiring breast!

So fades a summer cloud away,
So sinks the gale when storms are o'er;
So gently shuts, the eye of day,
So dies a wave along the shore.

A holy quiet reigns around,
A calm which life nor death destroys;
Nothing disturbs that peace profound,
Which his unfettered soul enjoys.

Farewell, conflicting hopes and fears,
Where lights and shades alternate dwell;
How bright the unchanging morn appears!
Farewell, inconstant world, farewell!

Life's duty done, as sinks the clay,
Light from its load the spirit flies;
While heaven and earth combine to say,
"How blest the righteous when he dies!"

132.   NAOMI.   C. M.

LIFE is a span, a fleeting hour,
  How soon the vapor flies!
Man is a tender, transient flower,
  That e'en in blooming dies.

Death spreads his withering, wintry arms,
  And beauty smiles no more;
Ah! where are now those rising charms,
  Which pleased our eyes before?

That once loved form, now cold and dead,
  Each mournful thought employs;
We weep, our earthly comforts fled,
  And withered all our joys.

Hope looks beyond the bounds of time,
  When what we now deplore,
Shall rise in full, immortal prime,
  And bloom to fade no more.

Cease, then, fond nature, cease thy tears;
    The Saviour dwells on high:
There everlasting spring appears,
    There joys shall never die.

133.   NOTTINGHILL.   C. M.

ALAS! how changed that lovely flower,
    Which bloomed and cheered my heart;
Fair, fleeting comfort of an hour,
    How soon we're called to part!

And shall my bleeding heart arraign
    That God, whose ways are love;
Or vainly cherish anxious pain
    For *her* who rests above?

No!—let me rather humble pay
    Obedience to his will,
And with my inmost spirit say,
    "The Lord is righteous still."

From adverse blasts, and lowering storms,
    Her favored soul he bore;
And with yon bright, angelic forms,
    She lives to die no more.

Why should I vex my heart, or fast?
    No more *she'll* visit me;
My soul will mount to *her* at last
    And there my child I'll see.

Prepare me, blessed Lord, to share
    The bliss thy people prove;
Who round thy glorious throne appear,
    And dwell in perfect love.

134.   DUNLAP'S CREEK. C. M.

THAT awful day will surely come,
    Th' appointed hour makes haste.
When I must stand before my Judge,
    And pass the solemn test,

Thou lovely Chief of all my joys,
    Thou Sovereign of my heart,
How could I bear to hear thy voice
    Pronounce the word, "Depart?"

O wretched state of deep despair,
    To see my God remove,
And fix my doleful station, where
    I must not taste his love.

Jesus, I throw my arms around,
    And hang upon thy breast;
Without a gracious smile from thee,
    My spirit cannot rest.

HEAVEN.

135.   WORLD OF LIGHT. IRR. M.

There is a beautiful world,
Where saints and angels sing,
A world where peace and pleasure reign,
And heavenly praises ring.
We'll be there, we'll be there,
Palms of victory, crowns of glory, we shall wear,
In that beautiful world on high.

There is a beautiful world,
Where sorrow never comes;
A world where tears shall never fall,
In sighing for our home.
We'll be there, we'll be there, &c.

There is a beautiful world,
Unseen to mortal sight;
And darkness never enters there;
That home is fair and bright.
We'll be there, we'll be there, &c.

There is a beautiful world,
Of harmony and love;
O may we safely enter there,
And dwell with God above.
We'll be there, we'll be there, &c.

136. MELROSE. C. M.

There is a land of pure delight,
  Where saints immortal reign;
Infinite day excludes the night,
  And pleasures banish pain.

There everlasting spring abides,
  And never withering flowers;
Death, like a narrow sea, divides
  This heavenly land from ours.

Sweet fields beyond the swelling flood,
  Stand dressed in living green;
So to the Jews old Canaan stood,
  While Jordan rolled between.

But timorous mortals start and shrink
  To cross this narrow sea;
And linger, shivering on the brink,
  And fear to launch away.

O could we make our doubts remove,
  Those gloomy doubts that rise,
And see the Canaan that we love
  With unbeclouded eyes:

Could we but climb where Moses stood,
  And view the landscape o'er,
Not Jordan's stream, nor death's cold flood,
  Should fright us from the shore.

137. "NO SORROW THERE," OR,
"NEARER HOME." S. M.

Far from my heavenly home,
  Far from my Father's breast,
Fainting, I cry, "Blest Spirit, come
  And speed me to thy rest!"

CHORUS.

‖: There'll be no sorrow there ::‖
In heaven above, where all is love,—
  There'll be no sorrow there.

Upon the willows long
  My harp has silent hung;
How should I sing a cheerful song,
  Till thou inspire my tongue?

My Spirit homeward turns,
  And fain would thither flee:
My heart, O Zion, droops and yearns,
  When I remember thee.

To thee, to thee I press—
  A dark and toilsome road;
When shall I pass the wilderness,
  And reach the saints' abode?

God of my life, be near;
  On thee my hopes I cast:
O guide me through the desert here,
  And bring me home at last!

138. SHINING SHORE. 8, 7.

My days are gliding swiftly by,
   And I, a pilgrim stranger,
Would not detain them as they fly,
   These hours of toil and danger:
For oh, we stand on Jordan's strand,
   Our friends are passing over,
And just before, the shining shore
   We may almost discover.

We'll gird our loins, my brethren dear,
   Our distant home discerning;
Our absent Lord has left us word,
   Let every lamp be burning;
For oh, we stand, &c.

Should coming days be cold and dark,
   We need not cease our singing;
That perfect rest naught can molest,
   When angel harps are ringing;
For oh, we stand, &c.

Let sorrow's rudest tempest blow,
   Each cord on earth to sever;
Our King says, "Come," and there's our home,
   For ever, oh, for ever!
For oh, we stand, &c.

139. LOOKING HOME. IRR. M.

Ah! this heart is void and chill,
    'Mid earth's noisy thronging;
For my Father's mansions still
    Earnestly is longing.
        Looking home, looking home,
        Tow'rds the heavenly mansions
        Jesus hath prepared for me,
        In his Father's kingdom.

Soon the glorious day will dawn,
    Heavenly pleasures bringing;
Night will be exchanged for morn,
    Sighs give place to singing.
        Looking home, &c.

Oh! to be at home again,
    All for which we're sighing,
From all earthly want and pain
    To be swiftly flying.
        Looking home, &c.

With this load of sin and care,
    Then no longer bending,
But with waiting angels there
    On our soul attending.
        Looking home, &c.

Blessed home, oh! blessed home,
    All for which we're sighing,

Soon our Lord will bid us come
To our Father's kingdom.
Looking home, &c.

140.   BROWN. C. M.

Jerusalem, my happy home,
  Name ever dear to me!
When shall my labors have an end,
  In joy, and peace, and thee?

When shall these eyes thy heaven-built walls
  And pearly gates behold?
Thy bulwarks, with salvation strong,
  And streets of shining gold?

O when, thou city of my God,
  Shall I thy courts ascend,
Where congregations ne'er break up,
  And Sabbaths have no end?

There happier bowers than Eden's bloom,
  Nor sin nor sorrow know:
Blest seats, through rude and stormy scenes,
  I onward press to you.

Why should I shrink at pain and woe,
  Or feel at death, dismay?
I've Canaan's goodly land in view,
  And realms of endless day.

Jerusalem, my happy home,
  My soul still pants for thee;
Then shall my labors have an end,
  When I thy joys shall see.

141. MELROSE. C. M.

When I can read my title clear,
  To mansions in the skies,
I bid farewell to every fear,
  And wipe my weeping eyes.

Should earth against my soul engage,
  And hellish darts be hurled,
Then I can smile at Satan's rage,
  And face a frowning world.

Let cares like a wild deluge come,
  And storms of sorrow fall;
May I but safely reach my home,
  My God, my heaven, my all.

There shall I bathe my weary soul
  In seas of heavenly rest,
And not a wave of trouble roll
  Across my peaceful breast.

142. NEARER HOME. S. M.

One sweetly solemn thought
  Comes to me o'er and o'er:
Nearer my home am I to-day
  Than e'er I have been before.
    Chorus.—There'll be no sorrow there.

Nearer my Father's house
  Where many mansions be;—
Nearer my Saviour's great white throne;
  Nearer the crystal sea;—

Nearer to reach the end
  And lay my burden down;
Nearer to leave my weary cross;
  Nearer to wear my crown.

But through that gloomy vale
  Where all is shade and night,
Flows on the deep and unknown stream,
  Between me and the light.

Father, perfect my trust;
  Strengthen my trembling faith;
Help me and hold me, when my feet
  Stand on the brink of death.

143. BETHANY. 6, 4.

Nearer, my God, to thee,
  Nearer to thee!
E'en though it be a cross
  That raiseth me,
Still all my song shall be,
Nearer, my God, to thee*
  Nearer to thee.

* Repeat the sixth line.

Though a lone wanderer,
　The sun gone down,
Darkness be over me,
　Pillowed on stone,
Yet in my dreams I'd be
Nearer, my God, to thee,
　Nearer to thee.

There let the way appear
　Steps up to heav'n,—
All that thou sendest me
　In mercy giv'n,—
Angels to beckon me
Nearer, my God, to thee,
　Nearer to thee.

Then, with my waking thoughts
　Bright with thy praise,
Out of my stony griefs
　Bethel I'll raise;
So by my woes to be
Nearer, my God, to thee,
　Nearer to thee.

Or, if on joyful wing
　Cleaving the sky,
Sun, moon, and stars forgot,
　Upward I fly,
Still all my song shall be,
Nearer, my God, to thee,
　Nearer to thee.

144. BETHANY. 6, 4

I'm but a stranger here,
  Heav'n is my home;
Earth is a desert drear,
  Heav'n is my home;
Dangers and sorrows stand
Round me on every hand,
Heav'n is my Father-land,
  Heav'n is my home.

What though the tempests rage,
  Heav'n is my home;
Short is my pilgrimage,
  Heav'n is my home;
And time's wild wintry blast
Soon will be overpast,
I shall reach home at last,—
  Heav'n is my home.

Therefore I murmur not,
  Heav'n is my home;
What e'er my earthly lot,
  Heav'n is my home;
And I shall surely stand
There at my Lord's right hand;
Heav'n is my Father-land,—
  Heav'n is my home.

145. NO SORROW THERE. S. M.

    Oh sing to me of heaven,
      When I am called to die;
    Sing songs of holy ecstasy
      To waft my soul on high.
      CHORUS.—There'll be no sorrow there.

    When cold and sluggish drops
      Roll off my marble brow,
    Break forth in sounds of joyfulness;
      Let heaven begin below.

    When the last moments come,
      Oh watch my dying face,
    To catch the bright seraphic gleam
      Which o'er my features plays.

    Then to my raptured ear
      Let one sweet song be given;
    Let music charm me last on earth,
      And greet me first in heaven.

146. "SWEET LAND OF REST." IRR. M.

    Sweet land of rest, for thee I sigh,
      When will the moment come,
    That I shall lay my armor by,
      And dwell with Christ at home?

      CHORUS.

    Home, home, sweet, sweet home!
      And dwell with Christ at home.

No tranquil joys on earth I know,
　No peaceful sheltering home;
This world's a wilderness of woe,
　This world is not my home.

To Jesus Christ I sought for rest,
　He bade me cease to roam,
But fly for succor to his breast,
　And he'd conduct me home.

When, by affliction sharply tried,
　I viewed the gaping tomb,
Although I dread death's chilling tide,
　Yet still I sighed for home.

Weary of wandering round and round
　This vale of sin and gloom,
I long to leave th' unhallowed ground,
　And dwell with Christ at home.

147.　　NO SORROW THERE.　　S. M.

FAR from these scenes of night
　Unbounded glories rise,
And realms of joy and pure delight
　Unknown to mortal eyes.

CHORUS.

‖:There'll be no sorrow there:‖
In heaven above, where all is love,—
　There'll be no sorrow there.

Fair land!—could mortal eyes
  But half its charms explore,
How would our spirits long to rise,
  And dwell on earth no more.

No cloud those regions know
  Realms ever bright and fair;
For sin the source of mortal woe,
  Can never enter there.

O may the prospect fire
  Our hearts with ardent love,
Till wings of faith, and strong desire,
  Bear every thought above.

148 THAT BEAUTIFUL LAND. IRR. M.

A BEAUTIFUL land by faith I see,
A land of rest from sorrow free,
The home of the ransomed, bright and fair,
And beautiful angels too are there.

CHORUS.

  Will you go? Will you go?
  Go to that beautiful land with me?
  Will you go? Will you go?
  Go to that beautiful land?

That beautiful land, the city of light,
It ne'er has known the shades of night:

The glory of God, the light of day
Hath driven the darkness far away.

In vision I see its streets of gold,
Its beautiful gates I too behold,
The river of life, the crystal sea,
The ambrosial fruit of life's fair tree.

The heavenly throng arrayed in white,
In rapture range the plains of light;
And in one harmonious choir they praise
Their glorious Saviour's matchless grace.

149.   GOING HOME. IRR. M.

My heavenly home is bright and fair,
Nor pain nor death can enter there;
Its glittering towers the sun outshine;
That heavenly mansion shall be mine.

CHORUS.

Will you go? Will you go?
Go to that heavenly home with me?
Will you go? Will you go?
Go to that heavenly home?

My Father's house is built on high,
Far, far above the starry sky:
When from this earthly prison free,
That heavenly mansion mine shall be.

Let others seek a home below,
Which flames devour, or waves o'erflow;

Be mine the happier lot to own
A heavenly mansion near the throne.

Then fail this earth, let stars decline,
And sun and moon refuse to shine,
All nature sink and cease to be,
That heavenly mansion stands for me.

150.   BEULAH.   IRR. M.

THERE is a happy land
  Far, far away,
Where saints in glory stand,
  Bright, bright as day;
Oh, how they sweetly sing,
Worthy is our Saviour King,
Loud let his praises ring,
  Praise, praise for aye.

Come to that happy land,
  Come, come away;
Why will ye doubting stand,
  Why still delay?
Oh, we shall happy be,
When, from sin and sorrow free,
Lord, we shall live with Thee,
  Blest, blest for aye.

Bright, in that happy land,
  Beams every eye;
Kept by a Father's hand,
  Love cannot die.

Oh then to glory run,
  Be a crown and kingdom won;
And bright above the sun,
  We reign for aye.

151.   AYRSHIRE.   8, 7.

BRIGHTLY gleams a holy radiance
  Round that undiscovered land,
Where immortal hopes are anchored,
  And immortal joys expand;
And that radiance pure and heav'nly,
  All undimmed by earthly bl'ght,
Is the shadow of Thy glory,—
  Thine the fountain of all light.

Darkness flees away before Thee,
  Sun and stars no more can shine,
And the angels who adore Thee
  Bow beneath those rays divine;
And through all the glorious city
  Thine is undivided might,—
Thou its pow'r, and life, and glory,
  Thou the temple and the light.

Angel harps, Thy praise attuning,
  Sing thy wondrous love to man;
Countless millions glad are shouting
  God Almighty and the Lamb!
The redeemed of every nation
  "Walk in light" with the I AM,

And the shining hosts cry glory,
  God Almighty and the Lamb!

152.   "NEARER HOME."   S. M.

"For ever with the Lord!"
  Amen. So let it be;
Life from the dead is in that word,
  'Tis immortality.
Here in the body pent,
  Absent from him I roam,
Yet nightly pitch my moving tent,
  A day's march nearer home.
  Nearer home, nearer home,
  A day's march nearer home.

My Father's house on high,
  Home of my soul, how near,
At times to faith's forseeing eye,
  Thy golden gates appear.
    Here in the body pent, &c.

Ah! then my spirit faints
  To reach the land I love,—
The bright inheritance of saints,
  Jerusalem above
    Here in the body pent, &c.

" For ever with the Lord!"
  —Father, if 'tis thy will,

The promise of that faithful word
　　Even here to me fulfil.
　　　Here in the body pent, &c.

153.　GREENVILLE, OR DISMISSION.
8, 7, 4.

Lord, dismiss us with thy blessing,
　　Fill our hearts with joy and peace,
Let us each, thy love possessing,
　　Triumph in redeeming grace;
　　　O refresh us,
　　Travelling through this wilderness.

Thanks we give and adoration,
　　For thy gospel's joyful sound,
May the fruits of thy salvation
　　In our hearts and lives abound;
　　　May thy presence
　　With us evermore be found.

So, whenever the signal's given,
　　Us from earth to call away;
Borne on angels' wings to heaven,
　　Glad to leave our cumbrous clay,
　　　May we ready,
　　Rise and reign in endless day.

MISCELLANEOUS.

THE LORD'S DAY, THE CHURCH, AND PUBLIC WORSHIP.

154.   LISBON. S. M.

Welcome, sweet day of rest,
  That saw the Lord arise,
Welcome to this reviving breast,
  And these rejoicing eyes.

The King Himself comes near,
  And feasts His Saints to-day;
Here we may sit, and see Him here,
  And love, and praise, and pray.

One day amidst the place
  Where my dear God hath been,
Is sweeter than ten thousand days
  Of pleasurable sin.

My willing soul would stay
  In such a frame as this,
And sit and sing herself away
  To everlasting bliss.

155. CHRISTMAS, or COLCHESTER. C. M.

Blest morning! whose first dawning light
  Beheld our rising God;

That saw Him triumph o'er the dust,
  And leave His last abode.

To Thy great name, almighty Lord,
  These sacred hours we pay,
And loud hosannas shall proclaim
  The triumph of the day

In the cold prison of the tomb,
  The dear Redeemer lay,
Till the revolving skies had brought
  The third, the appointed day.

Hell and the grave unite their force,
  To hold our God, in vain;
The sleeping Conqueror arose,
  And burst their feeble chain.

Salvation and immortal praise
  To our victorious King!
Let heaven and earth, and rocks and seas,
  With glad hosannas ring.

156. LENOX, OR LISCHER. H. M.

Welcome, delightful morn,
  Thou day of sacred rest,
We hail thy kind return,
  Lord, make these moments blessed;
From the low train of mortal toys
We soar to reach immortal joys.

Now may the King descend,
  And fill His throne of grace;
Thy sceptre, Lord, extend,
  While saints address Thy face;
Let sinners feel Thy quickening word,
And learn to know and fear the Lord.

Descend, celestial Dove,
  With all Thy quickening powers,
Disclose a Saviour's love,
  And bless these sacred hours;
Then shall our souls new life obtain,
Nor Sabbaths be bestowed in vain.

157. HEBRON, OR WARE, (GOLD'S). L. M.

Another six days' work is done,
Another Sabbath is begun;
Return, my soul, enjoy thy rest,
Improve the day thy God hath blessed.

O that our thoughts and thanks may rise
As grateful incense to the skies,
And draw from heaven that sweet repose,
Which none but he, that feels it knows.

This heavenly calm within the breast
Is the dear pledge of glorious rest,
Which for the church of God remains,
The end of cares, the end of pains.

In holy duties let the day,
In holy pleasures pass away;
How sweet a Sabbath thus to spend,
In hope of one that ne'er shall end!

158. ROCKBRIDGE, OR FOREST. L. M.

Far from my thoughts, vain world, begone,
Let my religious hours alone;
Fain would my eyes my Saviour see,
I wait a visit, Lord, from Thee.

O warm my heart with holy fire,
And kindle there a pure desire:
Come, my dear Jesus, from above,
And feed my soul with heavenly love.

Blest Jesus, what delicious fare,
How sweet Thine entertainments are!
Never did angels taste above
Redeeming grace and dying love.

159. HALL, OR OLNEY. S. M.

How charming is the place,
  Where my Redeemer God
Unveils the beauties of His face,
  And sheds His love abroad!

Here on the mercy-seat,
  With radiant glory crowned,
Our joyful eyes behold Him sit,
  And smile on all around.

To Him their prayers and cries
    All humbled souls present;
He listens to the broken sighs,
    And grants them all they want.

To them His sovereign will
    He graciously imparts,
And in return accepts with smiles
    The tribute of their hearts.

Give me, O Lord, a place
    Within Thy blest abode,
Among the children of Thy grace
    The servants of my God.

160.   LISBON. S. M.

I LOVE Thy kingdom, Lord,
    The house of Thine abode,
The church our blest Redeemer saved
    With His own precious blood.

I love Thy church, O God!
    Her walls before Thee stand,
Dear as the apple of Thine eye,
    And graven on Thy hand.

For her my tears shall fall,
    For her my prayers ascend,
To her my cares and toils be given
    Till toils and cares shall end.

Beyond my highest joy
  I prize her heavenly ways
Her sweet communion, solemn vows,
  Her hymns of love and praise.

161.   LENOX. H. M.

Lord of the worlds above,
  How pleasant and how fair
The dwellings of Thy love,
  Thy earthly temples are;
    To Thine abode
My heart aspires, with warm desires
    To see my God.

O happy souls that pray,
  Where God appoints to hear!
O happy men that pay
  Their constant service there!
    They praise thee still;
And happy they, that love the way
    To Zion's hill.

They go from strength to strength,
  Through this dark vale of tears,
Till each arrives at length,
  Till each in heaven appears;
    O glorious seat,
When God our King shall thither bring
    Our willing feet!

To spend one sacred day
  Where God and saints abide,

Affords diviner joy
  Than thousand days beside;
    Where God resorts,
I love it more to keep the door,
  Than shine in courts.

162, HOWARD OR CHRISTMAS. C. M.

Arise, O King of grace, arise,
  And enter to Thy rest;
Lo! Thy church waits with longing eyes
  Thus to be owned and blest.

Enter with all Thy glorious train,
  Thy Spirit and Thy word;
All that the ark did once contain
  Could no such grace afford.

Here, mighty God, accept our vows,
  Here let Thy praise be spread,
Bless the provisions of Thy house,
  And fill Thy poor with bread.

Here let the Son of David reign,
  Let God's Anointed shine,
Justice and truth His court maintain,
  With love and power divine.

Here let Him hold a lasting throne,
  And as His kingdom grows,
Fresh honors shall adorn His crown,
  And shame confound His foes.

163. MARLOW, OR DUNLAP'S CREEK. C. M.

Dear Shepherd of Thy people, here
  Thy presence now display;
As Thou hast given a place for prayer,
  So give us hearts to pray.

Show us some token of Thy love,
  Our fainting hope to raise,
And pour Thy blessing from above,
  That we may render praise.

Within these walls let holy peace,
  And love and concord dwell;
Here give the troubled conscience ease,
  The wounded spirit heal.

The feeling heart, the melting eye,
  The humbled mind bestow,
And shine upon us from on high,
  To make our graces grow.

May we in faith receive Thy word,
  In faith present our prayers,
And in the presence of our Lord,
  Unbosom all our cares.

And may the gospel's joyful sound,
  Enforced by mighty grace,
Awaken many sinners round,
  To come and fill the place.

GOSPEL MINISTRY.

164. OLD HUNDRED, OR PARK STREET.

L. M.

"Go, preach my gospel," saith the Lord,
"Bid the whole earth My grace receive;
He shall be saved who trusts My word,—
He shall be damned that won't believe.

"I'll make your great commission known,
And ye shall prove My gospel true,
By all the works that I have done,
By all the wonders ye shall do.

"Go, heal the sick, go, raise the dead,
Go, cast out devils in My name;
Nor let My prophets be afraid,
Though Greeks reproach, and Jews blaspheme.

"Teach all the nations My command,—
I'm with you till the world shall end;
All power is trusted to My hands,
I can destroy, and can defend."

He spake, and light shone round His head;
On a bright cloud to heaven He rode:
They to the farthest nations spread
The grace of their ascended God.

165. ST. THOMAS. S. M.

How beauteous are their feet,
  Who stand on Sion's hill,
Who bring salvation on their tongues,
  And words of peace reveal.

How charming is their voice!
  How sweet their tidings are!
"Sion, behold thy Saviour King,
  He reigns and triumphs here."

How happy are our ears,
  That hear this joyful sound,
Which kings and prophets waited for,
  And sought but never found!

How blessed are our eyes,
  That see this heavenly light!
Prophets and kings desired it long,
  But died without the sight.

The watchmen join their voice,
  And tuneful notes employ,
Jerusalem breaks forth in songs,
  And deserts learn the joy.

O Lord, make bare Thine arm
  Through all the earth abroad;
Let every nation now behold
  Their Saviour and their God.

MORNING.

166.   SILVER STREET.   S. M.

Behold, the morning sun
  Begins his glorious way,
His beams through all the nations run,
  And life and light convey.

But, where the gospel comes,
  It spreads diviner light;
It calls dead sinners from their tombs,
  And gives the blind their sight.

How perfect is Thy word,
  And all Thy judgments just;
For ever sure Thy promise, Lord,
  And men securely trust.

My gracious God, how plain
  Are Thy directions given!
Oh may I never read in vain,
  But find the path to heaven.

I hear Thy word with love,
  And I would fain obey;
Send Thy good Spirit from above
  To guide me, lest I stray.

167. EVAN, OR MELODY. C. M.

Lord, in the morning Thou shalt hear
  My voice ascending high;
To Thee will I direct my prayer,
  To Thee lift up mine eye:

Up to the hills where Christ is gone
  To plead for all His saints,
Presenting at His Father's throne
  Our songs and our complaints.

Thou art a God before whose sight
  The wicked shall not stand;
Sinners shall ne'er be Thy delight,
  Nor dwell at Thy right hand.

But to Thy house will I resort,
  To taste Thy mercies there;
I will frequent Thy holy court,
  And worship in Thy fear.

Oh may Thy Spirit guide my feet
  In ways of righteousness;
Make every path of duty straight
  And plain before my face.

THE BIBLE.

168. HARMONY GROVE, OR HERMON. C. M.

Father of mercies, in Thy word
  What endless glory shines!

For ever be Thy name adored,
  For these celestial lines.

Here may the wretched sons of want
  Exhaustless riches find;
Riches, above what earth can grant,
  And lasting as the mind.

Here the Redeemer's welcome voice
  Spreads heavenly peace around;
And life and everlasting joys
  Attend the blissful sound.

Oh may these heavenly pages be
  My ever dear delight;
And still new beauties may I see,
  And still increasing light.

Divine Instructor, gracious Lord,
  Be Thou for ever near;
Teach me to love Thy sacred word,
  And view my Saviour there.

169. WOODLAND, OR RISSAH. C. M.

How precious is the book divine,
  By inspiration given!
Bright as a lamp its doctrines shine,
  To guide our souls to heaven.

It sweetly cheers our drooping hearts,
  In this dark vale of tears;

Life, light and joy it still imparts,
  And quells our rising fears.

This lamp, through all the tedious night
  Of life, shall guide our way,—
Till we behold the clearer light
  Of an eternal day.

CHILDREN AND YOUTH.

170. BROWN, OR HERMON. C. M.

How shall the young secure their hearts,
  And guard their lives from sin?
Thy word the choicest rules imparts
  To keep the conscience clean.

When once it enters to the mind,
  It spreads such light abroad,
The meanest souls instruction find,
  And raise their thoughts to God.

The men that keep Thy law with care,
  And meditate Thy word,
Grow wiser than their teachers are,
  And better know the Lord.

Thy word is everlasting truth,
  How pure is every page!
That holy book shall guide our youth,
  And well support our age.

CHILDREN AND YOUTH. 147

171.   DUNDEE. C. M.

How large the promise, how divine,
   To Abraham and his seed!
"I'll be a God to thee and thine,
   Supplying all their need."

The words of His extensive love
   From age to age endure;
The Angel of the covenant proves
   And seals the blessings sure.

Jesus the ancient faith confirms
   To our great father given;
He takes young children in His arms,
   And calls them heirs of heaven.

Our God! how faithful are His ways;
   His love endures the same;
Nor from the promise of His grace
   Blots out the children's name.

172.   ROCKINGHAM, OR DUNLAP CREEK.
             C. M.

SEE Israel's gentle Shepherd stand
   With all-engaging charms;
Hark, how He calls the tender lambs,
   And folds them in His arms!

"Permit them to approach," He cries,
   "Nor scorn their humble name,

For 'twas to bless such souls as these,
   The Lord of angels came."

We bring them, Lord, in thankful hands,
   And yield them up to Thee;
Joyful that we ourselves are Thine,—
   Thine let our offspring be.

178.   STATE STREET.   S. M.

WITH humble heart and tongue,
   Our God, to Thee we pray,
Oh make us learn while we are young,
   How we may cleanse our way.

Make us, unguarded youth,
   The objects of Thy care,
Help us to choose the way of truth,
   And fly from every snare.

Our hearts to folly prone,
   Renew by power divine,
Unite them to Thyself alone,
   And make us wholly Thine.

Oh let Thy word of grace
   Our warmest thoughts employ,
Be this through all our foll'wing days,
   Our treasure and our joy.

To what Thy laws impart,
   Be our whole soul inclined;

Oh let them dwell within our heart,
  And sanctify our mind.

May Thy young servants learn,
  By these to cleanse their way;
And may we here the path discern
  That leads to endless day.

THE LORD'S SUPPER.

174. WINDHAM. L. M.

'Twas on that dark, that doleful night,
  When powers of earth and hell arose
Against the Son of God's delight,
  And friends betrayed Him to His foes.

Before the mournful scene began,
  He took the bread, and blessed, and brake;
What love through all His actions ran!
  What wondrous words of grace He spake!

"This is my body broke for sin,
  Receive and eat the living food;"
Then took the cup and blessed the wine,
  "'Tis the new covenant in My blood."

"Do this, (He cried,) till time shall end,
  In memory of your dying Friend;

Meet at My table, and record
  The love of your departed Lord."

Jesus, Thy feast we celebrate,
  We show Thy death, we sing Thy name,
Till Thou return, and we shall eat
  The marriage supper of the Lamb.

175. ORTONVILLE, OR ROCKINGHAM. C. M.

According to Thy gracious word,
  In meek humility,
This will I do, my dying Lord,
  I will remember Thee.

Thy body, broken for my sake,
  My bread from heaven shall be:
Thy testamental cup I take,
  And thus remember Thee.

Gethsemane can I forget,
  Or there Thy conflict see,
Thine agony and bloody sweat,
  And not remember Thee?

When to the cross I turn mine eyes,
  And rest on Calvary,
O Lamb of God, my sacrifice,
  I must remember Thee:

Remember Thee and all Thy pains,
  And all Thy love to me;

Yea, while a breath, a pulse remains,
 Will I remember Thee.

And when these failing lips grow dumb,
 And mind and memory flee,
When Thou shalt in Thy kingdom come,
 Jesus, remember me.

176. ASHFIELD, OR WINDHAM. L. M.

Deep in our hearts let us record
The deeper sorrows of our Lord;
Behold the rising billows roll
To overwhelm His holy soul.

In long complaints He spends His breath,
While hosts of hell, and powers of death,
And all the sons of malice join
To execute their curst design.

Yet, gracious God, Thy power and love
Have made the curse a blessing prove;
Those dreadful sufferings of Thy Son
Atoned for crimes which we had done.

The pangs of our expiring Lord
The honors of Thy law restored;
His sorrows made Thy justice known,
And paid for follies not His own.

Oh for his sake our guilt forgive,
And let the mourning sinner live;
The Lord will hear us in his name,
Nor shall our hope be turned to shame.

177. CRUCIFIX, (A GREEK MELODY,) OR
CANONBURY, 7, 6.

O SACRED Head, once wounded,
　With grief and pain weighed down,
How scornfully surrounded
　With thorns, Thine only crown!
How pale art Thou with anguish,
　With sore abuse and scorn!
How does that visage languish,
　Which once was bright as morn!

O Lord of life and glory,
　What bliss till now was Thine!
I read the wondrous story,
　I joy to call Thee mine.
Thy grief and Thy compassion
　Were all for sinners' gain;
Mine, mine was the transgression,
　But Thine the deadly pain.

What language shall I borrow
　To praise Thee, heav'nly Friend,—
For this Thy dying sorrow,
　Thy pity without end?
Lord, make me Thine forever,
　Nor let me faithless prove;
Oh let me never, never
　Abuse such dying love.

178. HORTON, OR ESHTEWOA, 7's.

Jesus, Master, hear me now,
While I would renew my vow,
And record Thy dying love;
Hear, and help me from above.

Feed me, Saviour, with this bread,
Broken in Thy body's stead;
Cheer my spirit with this wine,
Streaming like that blood of Thine.

And as now I eat and drink,
Let me truly, sweetly think,
Thou didst hang upon the tree,
Broken, bleeding, there—for me.

179. ARLINGTON. C. M.

Jesus, with all Thy saints above
 My tongue would bear her part,
Would sound aloud Thy saving love,
 And sing Thy bleeding heart.

Blest be the Lamb, my dearest Lord,
 Who bought me with His blood,
And quenched His Father's flaming sword
 In His own vital flood.

All glory to the dying Lamb,
 And never ceasing praise,

While angels live to know His name,
  Or saints to feel His grace.

180.   GROTON.   C. M.

Jesus, immortal King, arise!
  Rise and assert Thy sway;
Till earth, subdued, its tribute bring;
  And distant lands obey.

Ride forth, victorious conqueror! ride,
  Till all Thy foes submit;
And all the powers of hell resign
  Their trophies at Thy feet.

Send forth Thy word, and let it fly,
  This spacious earth around;
Till every soul beneath the sun,
  Shall hear the joyful sound.

From sea to sea, from shore to shore,
  May Jesus be adored;
And earth, with all her millions shout,—
  Hozanna to the Lord.

DOXOLOGIES.

L. M.

PRAISE God from whom all blessings flow;
Praise him, all creatures here below;
Praise him above, ye heavenly host:
Praise Father, Son, and Holy Ghost.

C. M.

LET God, the Father, and the Son,
And Spirit be adored,
Where there are works to make him known,
Or Saints to love the Lord.

S. M.

YE angels round the throne,
And Saints that dwell below,
Worship the Father and the Son,
And Holy Spirit too.

INDEX OF FIRST LINES.

	PAGE
A BEAUTIFUL LAND, BY FAITH I SEE	127
According to Thy gracious word	150
Arise, oh King of grace, arise	139
Ah! wretched souls, who strive in vain	74
Ah! this heart is void and chill	119
Alas! how changed that lovely flower	113
Alas! and did my Saviour bleed	22
All hail the power of Jesus' name	4
Am I a soldier of the Cross?	80
Amazing grace! how sweet the sound	67
Another six days' work is done	135
And can I yet delay?	58
Approach, my soul, the mercy seat	47
Arise, oh King of grace, arise	139
Awake, my soul, in joyful lays	89
Awake, my soul, stretch every nerve	90
Awaked by Sinai's awful sound	56
BEHOLD THE MORNING SUN	143
Blest be the tie that binds	78
Blest morning whose first dawning light	133
Brightly gleams a holy radiance	130
Brother, hast thou wandered far?	44
Behold, a stranger at the door	34
CHILD OF SIN AND SORROW	35
Come, Holy Spirit, Come	25
Come, Holy Spirit, heavenly Dove	24
Come, let us join our cheerful songs	75
Come, let us join our friends above	78
Come, my soul, thy suit prepare	81
Come, said Jesus' sacred voice	36
Come, sacred Spirit, from above	27
Come, humble sinner, in whose breast	42
Come, ye sinners, poor and wretched	37
Come, thou Fount of every blessing	99

	PAGE
DARK WAS THE NIGHT, AND COLD WAS THE GROUND	15
Dear Shepherd of Thy people, here	140
Deep in our hearts let us record	151
Dearest of all the names above	10
Delay not, delay not, O, sinner, draw near	36
Depth of mercy, can there be	52
Did Christ o'er sinners weep?	16
Didst thou, dear Jesus, suffer shame?	11
Dread Sovereign, let my evening song	101
FADE, FADE EACH EARTHLY JOY	94
Far from these scenes of night	126
Far from my heavenly home	117
Far from my thoughts, vain world begone	136
Father, I stretch my hands to thee	64
Father of mercies, in thy word	144
For ever with the Lord	131
From the cross, uplifted high	19
From Greenland's icy mountains	105
GENTLY, LORD, OH! GENTLY LEAD US	100
Glorious things of thee are spoken	104
"Go preach my gospel," saith the Lord	141
HEAR WHAT THE VOICE FROM HEAVEN PROCLAIMS	110
Here, at thy cross, incarnate God	62
Hail to the Lord's Anointed	106
Holy Father, thou hast taught us	85
Holy Ghost, with light divine	26
How oft, alas! this wretched heart	79
How blest the righteous when he dies	111
How beauteous are their feet	142
How charming is the place	136
How large the promise, how divine	147
How precious is the book divine	145
How shall the young secure their hearts	146
How happy are they	68
How sweet the name of Jesus sounds	5
How sad our state by nature is	71
I HEARD THE VOICE OF JESUS SAY	63

	PAGE
I'm not ashamed to own my Lord...................	72
I love to steal awhile away........................	100
I love thy kingdom, Lord...........................	137
I'm but a stranger here............................	124
I lay my sins on Jesus.............................	59
I saw One hanging on the tree.....................	13
I was a wandering sheep...........................	83
I was a traitor doomed to die.....................	55
JESUS, LOVER OF MY SOUL...........................	15
Jesus, I my cross have taken......................	92
Jesus, full of all compassion......................	20
Jesus, I love thy charming name...................	12
Jesus, thou art the sinner's friend................	65
Jesus, who knows full well.........................	82
Jesus, save my dying soul.........................	54
Jesus, Master, hear me now.......................	153
Jesus, immortal King, arise........................	154
Jesus, with all thy saints above...................	153
Jesus, and shall it ever be?.......................	73
Jesus, my all to heaven is gone...................	66
Jerusalem, my happy home.......................	120
Joy to the world! the Lord is come................	3
Just as I am, without one plea....................	60
LAMB OF GOD! WHOSE BLEEDING LOVE...............	91
Let every mortal ear attend.......................	31
Life is a span, a fleeting hour.....................	112
Like sheep we went astray........................	21
Lo! on a narrow neck of land.....................	57
Lord, behold us, few and weak....................	28
Lord, I hear the showers of blessing..............	52
Lord, in the morning thou shalt hear.............	144
Lord of the worlds above..........................	138
Lord, dismiss us with thy blessing................	132
MERCY ALONE CAN MEET MY CASE.....................	48
Must Jesus bear the cross alone..................	86
My days are gliding swiftly by....................	118
My heavenly home is bright and fair.............	128
My God, my Father, blissful name!................	93

INDEX OF FIRST LINES.

	PAGE
My God, my Father, while I stray	77
My soul, be on thy guard	82
My times of sorrow and of joy	97
NATURE WITH OPEN VOLUME STANDS	17
Nearer, my God, to thee	122
Not all the blood of beasts	14
Now begin the heavenly theme	90
Now is the accepted time	42
Now the Saviour standeth pleading	39
Now be the gospel banner	108
O! COULD I SPEAK THE MATCHLESS WORTH	8
O, for a closer walk with God	76
O, for a thousand tongues	5
O, for the death of those	109
O, happy day, that fixed my choice	66
O, Lord, thy work revive	29
O, sing to me of heaven	125
O thou that hearest the prayer of faith	69
O thou whose tender mercy hears	51
O thou that hearest when sinners cry	46
O whither should I go?	49
O what amazing words of grace!	33
One sweetly solemn thought	121
One there is, above all others	11
O, how I love thy holy law	93
O, God of Bethel, by whose hand	97
O sacred head, once wounded	152
PEOPLE OF THE LIVING GOD	70
Plunged in a gulf of dark despair	18
Prostrate, dear Jesus, at thy feet	50
RETURN, O WANDERER, TO THY HOME	41
Return, O wanderer, return	40
Rock of Ages, cleft for me	7
SAVIOUR, BREATHE AN EVENING BLESSING	102
Saviour, like a Shepherd lead us	98
Saviour, visit thy plantation	27

INDEX OF FIRST LINES.

	PAGE
Say, sinner, hath a voice within	39
See Israel's gentle Shepherd stand	147
Sinners, turn, why will ye die?	43
Show pity, Lord. O, Lord, forgive	53
Sion's King shall reign victorious	103
Soon may the last glad song arise	107
Sweet the moments, rich in blessing	87
Sweet land of rest for thee I sigh	125
Stay, thou insulted spirit, stay	46
THAT AWFUL DAY WILL SURELY COME	114
Take me, O, my Father, take me	60
The Lord's my Shepherd, I'll not want	96
The Spirit in our hearts	45
The Saviour! O, what endless charms!	9
The Saviour calls, let every ear	30
There is a land of pure delight	116
There is a happy land	129
There is no name so sweet	6
There is a beautiful world	115
There is a Fountain filled with blood	23
To-day the Saviour calls	33
To our Redeemer's glorious name	88
Triumphant Zion! lif thy head	107
'Tis a point I long to know	84
'Twas on that dark, that doleful night	149
UNVEIL THY BOSOM, FAITHFUL TOMB	110
WELCOME, DELIGHTFUL MORN	134
Welcome, sweet day of rest	133
When I can read my title clear	121
When rising from the bed of death	75
When I survey the wondrous cross	21
With tearful eyes I look around	49
With humble heart and tongue	143
YE WHO IN HIS COURTS ARE FOUND	32
Ye wretched, hungry, starving souls	31

THE END.

www.ingramcontent.com/pod-product-compliance
Lightning Source LLC
Chambersburg PA
CBHW030257170426

43202CB00009B/785